WILLIAMS-SONOMA

New American Cooking

The Pacific Northwest

GENERAL EDITOR **Chuck Williams**

RECIPES AND TEXT **Jean Galton**

FOOD PHOTOGRAPHY **Leigh Beisch**

TIME
LIFE
BOOKS

New Ameri

The Pacific Northwest

The

California

The Southwest

Table of **Contents**

Introduction

On my first visit to Seattle's Pike Place Market, I slowly worked my way through the crowd, past rows of glistening fish and pyramids of vegetables. I came to a berry vendor, his table an irresistible sea of inky blackberries. I bought as many cartons as I could carry. When I proudly showed off my purchase to some local friends, they laughed mercilessly. "You mean you actually bought blackberries?" they asked. I soon learned that here, in the Northwest, berry bushes overtake every empty lot and backyard corner. In other words, berries are to be picked, not purchased.

But berries are only the crowning jewels of the Pacific Northwest table, a cuisine blessed with a wondrous array of ingredients. With a maritime bounty ranging from salmon to Dungeness crab and a forest harvest that includes prized porcini and truffles, the Northwest harbors abundant culinary resources. The region's diverse climate is matched by an equally diverse range of growing conditions. The result is a wide variety of local products, from Washington State's famous apples, Oregon's noted wines, and Idaho's signature potatoes to buttery hazelnuts (filberts) and crimson cherries. For a Pacific Northwest cook to be successful, all that he or she needs are the freshest local ingredients. A saying of the Northwest Haida tribe may put it best: "When the tide is out, the table is set."

A Diverse Population

The Haida were just one of the many Native American tribes to populate the fertile Northwest, all of whom thrived for centuries before the arrival of white settlers. Living well on the region's wild roots and greens, small and large game, and, of course, fish, notably salmon and shellfish, the native peoples were highly self-reliant. By using wood smoke to preserve food for the winter, Northwest tribes survived the colder months with a full storehouse. Today, alder-smoked salmon continues to be an integral part of Northwest tradition.

The first white settlers to arrive in the Northwest were English trappers and fur traders in the early 1800s. But by the middle of the century, others had come, some traveling by boat, some by wagon train across the mountain passes. German Americans brought their beer and sausage, Italian Americans their olives and tomatoes. Sheep-herding Basques put down roots, and British and Scandinavian settlers took up logging and fishing. Chinese and Japanese worked the mines, helped to build the railroads, and served as laborers and cooks in canneries and the many logging camps.

Today, new populations continue to arrive. Waves of Asian immigrants, including Vietnamese, Koreans, Laotians, and Thais, have all settled here in recent decades, bringing their love of cilantro (fresh coriander), colorful basils, exotic greens, chiles, and ginger. Recent émigrés from Russia and from Latin America have brought their blini and *pupusas*. This tremendous assortment of flavors, from both old and new residents, has been woven into the fabric of Pacific Northwest cuisine. Today, cilantro may be paired with Italian pasta and fresh salmon, or a tortilla may be stuffed with Thai chicken and jasmine rice. Simply put, a wealth of ethnic ingredients and traditions is represented here, utilized by weekend cooks and professional chefs alike. In the early 1990s this innovative cross-ing of culinary borders was dubbed "fusion food." Today, it has become an everyday element of Pacific Northwest cooking.

A Varied Landscape

To understand the region fully, however, one must also explore its geography. The Cascade Mountains, home to some of the highest peaks in the nation, form a north-south divide. West of the Cascades lie

the Pacific Ocean and its attendant coastline, a fertile lowland stretch-ing from southwest Oregon through both Oregon and Washington and punctuated by the Olympic Moun-tains in northern Washington. The Strait of Juan de Fuca borders the area on the north and flows into Puget Sound, as well as into numerous other saltwater bays and waterways.

This entire lowland receives heavy rainfall—enough to qualify

it as a temperate rainforest. The precipitation keeps the area cool and moist, making it prime territory for dairy farming and for bumper crops of wild mushrooms and berries. In Oregon, this moist marine climate is tempered some-what, creating a perfect region for growing grapes, hazelnuts, and tree fruits. The Pacific Ocean delivers a bounty that includes oysters, mussels, clams, Dungeness crabs, shrimp (prawns), scallops, geoduck

Salmon, processed in a variety of ways (opposite), is central to the cuisine of the Pacific Northwest. Gai lan (left) is a prime example of the Asian influence in the region, as well as the exceptional vegetables to be found there.

clams, octopus, squid, petrale sole, Pacific cod, lingcod, black cod, halibut, sand dabs, rockfish, and five varieties of wild salmon.

The mighty Columbia River runs in a jagged line from the northeast corner of Washington southwest along the Oregon border. Flowing into the Pacific, the river is an important thoroughfare for

Pacific salmon, river smelt, and mild white sturgeon.

At one time largely desert, eastern Washington and Oregon, as well as parts of western Idaho, are now irrigated, transforming what was once dust into rich farmland. Long, hot summer days make the area ideal for growing tree fruits (apples, pears, apricots, and cherries), grapes, potatoes, Walla Walla onions, dry peas, lentils, and wheat. Hops, used in large quantities in Northwest microbreweries, come from eastern Washington as well.

A West Coast Movement

A diverse population and a varied landscape have helped contribute to the reputation the entire West Coast enjoys as a source of innovation. The growth in artisan foods represents just one of the new coastal movements. Although the seeds of this culinary revolution may have been sown in California, they have blossomed in the Pacific

Northwest, too. Nowhere else in the United States can one find so large a concentration of rustic-bread bakeries, premium wineries, microbreweries, and coffee roasters. Chocolatiers such as Fran's Choc-olates of Washington State create excellent confections featuring local ingredients. Carefully farmed oysters, mussels, and clams and the finest and freshest fish fill the display cases of fussy fishmongers. Chukar Dried Cherries and superb Sally Jackson Cheeses are pas-sionately produced by small, local companies. Their efforts have been well rewarded. Consumers and restaurateurs appreciate and sup-port these wonderful handmade products, and the demand only increases with each passing year.

Pacific Northwest cuisine is, in a word, simplicity. It is built on fresh ingredients of nearly unparalleled quality that require few culinary frills in the kitchen. When we allow these regional products to shine, Northwest cooking is at its best.

In the past, Northwest ingre-dients were too often taken for granted, with little or no thought given to the future. Today, locals are driven by a strong mandate to save the once bountiful marine life and precious forest resources and to practice sustainable-farming methods. Such critical actions give hope to the possibility that coming generations will be able to feast at our unique Pacific Northwest table.

Dungeness crab, a North-west staple, flavors a simple pasta sauce (opposite). Locally produced coffee, chocolate, and preserves (above) are examples of the Pacific Northwest's famed artisan foods.

ESPRESSO TO GO

1 Soups, Salads & Starters

Any one of these first-course recipes offers a substantial amount of food, enough to begin a traditional dinner or to enjoy with cocktails. But nowadays, the Northwest dining trend is toward smaller meals, and by combining two or three of these dishes, you will have put together a satisfying repast. Pair the Fresh Pea Soup with Crab and Mint (page 20) with the Poached Egg and Chanterelle Salad (page 28), or try the Spicy Cumin Walnuts (page 34), Matsutake and Napa Cabbage Pot Stickers (page 22), and the Peppered Salmon Trout and Plum Salad (page 33). The combinations are many and varied, and the wealth of tastes sparkles on the palate. But best of all, the dishes celebrate a parade of wonderful Northwest ingredients.

Salt-Grilled Smelts

24 smelts, about ¾ lb (375 g) total weight

1 teaspoon coarse salt

MAYONNAISE

½ cup (4 fl oz/125 ml) mayonnaise

2 tablespoons reduced-sodium soy sauce

½ teaspoon Asian sesame oil

pinch of cayenne pepper

1 green (spring) onion, minced

The smelt is a small, slender fish about the size of an anchovy. In the late spring, huge schools of smelts surge up the Columbia River to spawn. Local fishermen use dip nets to scoop up the sweet, silvery fish, while savvy cooks fire up their grills in anticipation of a good catch.

1. Prepare a hot fire on a charcoal grill, or preheat a gas or electric grill.

2. To clean each smelt, pinch the gills on both sides of the head and pull. (This will pull out the gills and innards. Alternatively, snap back the head and pull it off with the gills and innards.) Rinse the fish inside and out and pat dry. Sprinkle all the fish evenly on both sides with the salt.

3. To make the mayonnaise, in a small bowl, stir together the mayonnaise, soy sauce, sesame oil, and cayenne pepper. Set aside.

4. Oil a large grill basket or 2 smaller baskets and arrange the smelts in the basket(s). (If you do not have grill baskets, generously oil the grill rack.) Place the smelts over the fire and grill, turning once, until lightly browned and crisp, about 2 minutes on each side.

5. Transfer the smelts to a warmed platter or individual plates and sprinkle with the green onion. Pass the mayonnaise at the table.

SERVES 4

NUTRITIONAL ANALYSIS PER SERVING
Calories 253 (Kilojoules 1,063); Protein 9 g; Carbohydrates 2 g; Total Fat 24 g; Saturated Fat 4 g; Cholesterol 49 mg; Sodium 853 mg; Dietary Fiber 0 g

Fresh Pea Soup with Crab and Mint

2 tablespoons unsalted butter

6 green (spring) onions, thinly sliced

2 cups (10 oz/315 g) shelled fresh or frozen English peas

2½ cups (20 fl oz/625 ml) water

½ teaspoon coarse salt

½ teaspoon freshly ground pepper

2 tablespoons chopped fresh mint

5 oz (155 g) fresh-cooked Dungeness crabmeat, picked over for shell fragments

organic edible blossoms such as violets or nasturtiums (optional)

This soup is equally wonderful made with fresh or frozen peas. For variety, use lemon balm in place of the mint. Edible blossoms make a lovely garnish.

1. In a large saucepan over medium-high heat, melt 1 tablespoon of the butter. Add the green onions and sauté until wilted, 3–4 minutes. Stir in the peas, water, salt, and pepper and bring to a boil. Reduce the heat to medium-low, cover, and simmer until the peas are tender, about 5 minutes. Remove from the heat.

2. Using an immersion blender, purée the soup until smooth. Alternatively, scoop out the peas with a slotted spoon, place in a blender or food processor, and purée until smooth, adding a little of the cooking liquid if necessary. Return the purée to the pan. Stir in the mint.

3. Meanwhile, in a frying pan, melt the remaining 1 tablespoon butter over medium heat. Add the crabmeat and cook gently until warmed through, about 1 minute.

4. Ladle the soup into warmed bowls. Top each serving with some of the crabmeat and a few of the flowers, if using. Serve immediately.

SERVES 4

NUTRITIONAL ANALYSIS PER SERVING
Calories 153 (Kilojoules 643); Protein 12 g; Carbohydrates 12 g; Total Fat 7 g; Saturated Fat 4 g; Cholesterol 51 mg; Sodium 291 mg; Dietary Fiber 4 g

Matsutake and Napa Cabbage Pot Stickers

2 teaspoons plus 6 tablespoons (3 fl oz/90 ml) canola oil

4 cups (12 oz/375 g) finely shredded napa cabbage

¼ lb (125 g) fresh matsutake, shiitake, or other cultivated or wild mushrooms, wiped clean, tough stems removed, and thinly sliced

1 tablespoon peeled and shredded fresh ginger

2 green (spring) onions, coarsely chopped

1 carrot, peeled and shredded

2 tablespoons tamari

1 teaspoon Asian sesame oil

½ teaspoon freshly ground pepper

¼ teaspoon coarse salt

½ cup (3 oz/90 g) finely diced extra-firm tofu

1 package (12 oz/375 g) pot sticker wrappers

1 cup (8 fl oz/240 ml) water

DIPPING SAUCE

½ teaspoon Vietnamese chile-garlic sauce

3 tablespoons unseasoned rice vinegar

3 tablespoons firmly packed brown sugar

Matsutake mushrooms are white, thickly stemmed wild specimens prized in particular by the Japanese in both Japan and the Pacific Northwest. Since they are only available in the fall, fresh shiitake or cremini mushrooms, or a combination, can be substituted the rest of the year.

1. In a large frying pan over medium-high heat, warm 2 teaspoons canola oil. Add the cabbage and cook, stirring, until it wilts, about 2 minutes. Stir in the mushrooms, ginger, green onions, carrot, tamari, sesame oil, pepper, and salt and cook, stirring frequently, until the mushrooms are tender, about 4 minutes longer. Stir in the tofu and remove from the heat.

2. Line 2 baking sheets with parchment (baking) paper. On a work surface, lay out 6 pot sticker wrappers. Place a heaping teaspoonful of the cabbage filling in the center of each wrapper. Dip your finger in water and run it lightly around the edge of the wrapper. Fold each wrapper over to make a half-circle, enclosing the filling completely and pleating the edges firmly together. Transfer to a parchment-lined baking sheet. Repeat with the remaining filling and wrappers.

3. To make the dipping sauce, in a small bowl, stir together the chile-garlic sauce, rice vinegar, and brown sugar. Set aside.

4. Place a large, heavy frying pan over medium-high heat. When it is hot, add 2 tablespoons of the canola oil and heat until very hot but not smoking. Add about one-third of the pot stickers, seam side up, and cook until the bottoms are browned, 1–2 minutes. Add ⅓ cup (3 fl oz/80 ml) of the water—stand back, it splatters—cover, and simmer until tender, about 2 minutes. Using a slotted spoon, transfer the pot stickers to a warmed platter. Discard the water in the pan and repeat with the remaining pot stickers in two batches, using 2 tablespoons oil and ⅓ cup (3 fl oz/80 ml) water with each batch. Serve the pot stickers hot with the dipping sauce.

MAKES ABOUT 40 POT STICKERS; SERVES 8

NUTRITIONAL ANALYSIS PER SERVING
Calories 278 (Kilojoules 1,168); Protein 7 g; Carbohydrates 33 g; Total Fat 13 g; Saturated Fat 1 g; Cholesterol 4 mg; Sodium 555 mg; Dietary Fiber 3 g

R ain is the lifeblood of the wild mushroom. Thanks to the generous annual waterings our Pacific Northwest forests receive, the woodlands sprout a dazzling bounty of mushrooms.

Mushrooming has long been a part of Northwest history, practiced first by the Native Americans and then later by the early white settlers. Today, mushroom hunting is on the rise, fueled by the Northwesterner's love for the outdoors and by the high prices paid at market for matsutakes, morels, truffles, and porcini. Esteemed Northwest food writer Angelo Pellegrini has said that mushroom hunters are different from other hunters: "When stalking the mushroom, he has no other interests, passions, or feelings save an insatiable greed for the quarry."

But it's unwise to scour the forest floor yourself unless you're a true expert who can tell safe from toxic varieties. Morels, chanterelles, porcini, puffballs, shaggy manes, matsutakes, truffles, and hen-of-the-woods are just some of the wild mushrooms you are likely to find at farmers' markets and grocery stores. And most of the Northwest's fine restaurants cook with local mushrooms as a matter

Wild **Mushrooms**

of course. At the Joel Palmer House in Dayton, Oregon, chef-owner Jack Czarnecki specializes in mushrooms, doing most of the foraging himself for the restaurant's needs. Mushrooms are well-represented throughout the menu, from a first course of wontons stuffed with matsutakes to a dessert of cheesecake topped with a dried candy cap of mushroom syrup.

Sautéed Pea Shoots with Singing Scallops

3 tablespoons unsalted butter

1½ lb (750 g) pea shoots, rinsed but not dried

½ teaspoon salt

½ teaspoon freshly ground pepper

2 shallots, finely chopped

16 singing scallops in the shell, well rinsed, or 1 lb (500 g) other scallops

¼ cup (2 fl oz/60 ml) dry white wine

3 tablespoons finely diced tomato

2 tablespoons finely chopped mixed fresh herbs such as flat-leaf (Italian) parsley, mint, and thyme

1 teaspoon grated lemon zest

Singing scallops, delicately flavored bivalves, get their whimsical name because their pretty pink shells gape open. They're widely available in the Northwest, retrieved from the ocean floor by divers. If they're not available, you can use bay or sea scallops without the shells. They will take slightly less time to cook; add the remaining ingredients at the same time as you add the scallops.

1. In a large frying pan over medium-high heat, melt 1 tablespoon of the butter. Add the damp pea shoots and ¼ teaspoon each of the salt and pepper. Cover and cook, stirring occasionally, until wilted, 1–2 minutes. Uncover and transfer to individual plates. Keep warm.

2. Return the pan to medium-high heat and add 1 tablespoon of the remaining butter. When it melts, add the shallots and cook, stirring frequently, until soft, 2–3 minutes. Stir in the scallops and cook for 1 minute. Add the wine, tomato, herbs, lemon zest, and the remaining ¼ teaspoon each salt and pepper and 1 tablespoon butter. Simmer until the scallops are opaque throughout, about 1 minute.

3. Spoon the scallop mixture over the pea shoots and serve immediately.

SERVES 4

NUTRITIONAL ANALYSIS PER SERVING
Calories 411 (Kilojoules 1,726); Protein 34 g; Carbohydrates 52 g; Total Fat 11 g; Saturated Fat 6 g; Cholesterol 61 mg; Sodium 510 mg; Dietary Fiber 0 g

Roasted Oysters with Leeks and Sorrel

24 small or medium oysters in the shell

1 bunch sorrel, about 2 oz (60 g), stems removed

2 tablespoons unsalted butter

1 large leek, including about 2 inches (5 cm) of pale green, finely shredded

1½ teaspoons grated lemon zest

1½ teaspoons grated orange zest

½ teaspoon coarse salt

½ teaspoon freshly ground pepper

⅓ cup (3 fl oz/80 ml) heavy (double) cream

1 tablespoon chopped fresh flat-leaf (Italian) parsley

Oyster fans fall into two camps: those who eat them raw and those who prefer them lightly cooked. For the latter group, these roasted oysters make an elegant first course.

1. Working with 1 oyster at a time, and holding it over a bowl to capture the liquor (liquid), grip each shell, flat side up, with a folded kitchen towel. Push the tip of an oyster knife to one side of the hinge and pry upward to open the shell. Keeping the blade edge against the inside of the top shell, run the knife all around the oyster to sever the muscle that holds the shell halves together. Lift off and discard the top shell. Run the knife underneath the oyster to cut its flesh free from the bottom shell and set the oyster aside. Pour off the liquor from the shell into the bowl. Scrub the bottom shell with a stiff-bristled brush and place on a baking sheet lined with rumpled aluminum foil. When all the bottom shells are on the baking sheet, set an oyster in each shell. Cover and refrigerate until needed. Pour the oyster liquor through a fine-mesh sieve lined with cheesecloth (muslin) set over a small bowl and set aside.

2. Cut the sorrel leaves into a chiffonade: Working in batches, stack the leaves, tightly roll up the stack lengthwise and thinly slice the cylinder crosswise. Set aside. Preheat the oven to 450°F (230°C).

3. In a frying pan over medium heat, melt the butter. Add the leek and cook, stirring occasionally, until very soft, about 5 minutes. Add the sorrel and cook, stirring frequently, until soft, about 5 minutes. Stir in the lemon and orange zests, salt, pepper, cream, and strained liquor. Raise the heat to high and simmer until the liquid is reduced slightly, about 2 minutes. Remove from the heat and top each oyster with a tablespoon of the mixture. Spoon any remaining liquid over the oysters.

4. Bake the oysters until they are bubbling, 9–10 minutes. Divide among individual plates, sprinkle with the parsley, and serve.

SERVES 4

NUTRITIONAL ANALYSIS PER SERVING
Calories 190 (Kilojoules 798); Protein 6 g; Carbohydrates 10 g; Total Fat 15 g; Saturated Fat 8 g; Cholesterol 75 mg; Sodium 268 mg; Dietary Fiber 1 g

M ost folks driving through Willapa Bay, Washington, would see it as a typical coastal town. But oyster lovers like me will spot the local processors, nondescript warehouses flanked by enormous piles of spent oyster shells. The plump meats taken from those sun-bleached casings probably ended up in a bisque or stew, in a mixed-seafood fry or a three-egg omelet.

In 1850, at the height of the California gold rush, oysters fresh from Willapa Bay were crated and placed aboard schooners bound for San Francisco. The bivalves were an immediate hit, and, before long, as many as two hundred thousand bushels were being shipped each year. By 1895, the native oyster beds were nearly wiped out.

The first efforts to restore the depleted beds failed miserably. But in 1920, plantings of Japanese seed oysters took, and Willapa Bay was, once again, back in business.

These days, several varieties of both cupped and flat oysters are farmed. The most plentiful are the Pacific oysters, cupped specimens that bear the names of their farm

Northwest **Oysters**

locations, such as Yaquina, Wescott, Quilcene, and Shoalwater Bays. A second cupped oyster, the Kumamoto, is a tiny Japanese transplant treasured for its sweet taste. Farmed flat oysters include the native Olympia and the European flat, incredibly slow growers that are perfectly delicious raw with only a spritz of lemon juice.

Poached Egg and Chanterelle Salad

6 tablespoons (3 fl oz/90 ml) extra-virgin olive oil

1 tablespoon fresh lemon juice

¾ teaspoon coarse salt

¾ teaspoon freshly ground pepper

2 bunches watercress, tough stems removed

4 large slices artisan bread, each ½ inch (12 mm) thick

¾ lb (375 g) fresh chanterelle or other wild or cultivated mushrooms such as oyster, cremini, or porto-bello, rinsed quickly or wiped clean, and halved if large

1 tablespoon chopped fresh flat-leaf (Italian) parsley

4 eggs

Chanterelles are beautiful wild or cultivated mushrooms with ruffled tops and a distinctive woodsy flavor. They come in several colors, but the yellow chanterelle is the most common. If they are very dirty, rinse them quickly and pat dry.

1. Preheat the broiler (griller).

2. In a jar, combine 3 tablespoons of the olive oil, the lemon juice, and ¼ teaspoon each of the salt and pepper. Cover and shake well.

3. Place the watercress in a bowl. Drizzle with 2 tablespoons of the dressing and toss well. Divide among individual plates.

4. Brush the bread slices on both sides with 1 tablespoon of the oil and place on a baking sheet. Slip under the broiler and toast, turning once, until golden brown, about 1 minute on each side. Cut in half and set aside.

5. In a large frying pan over medium-high heat, warm the remaining 2 tablespoons olive oil. Add the mushrooms and sauté until tender, 3–5 minutes. Season with the remaining ½ teaspoon each salt and pepper, and add the parsley. Toss, remove from the heat, and keep warm.

6. Meanwhile, pour water into a shallow saucepan or sauté pan to a depth of 2 inches (5 cm) and bring to just under a boil. One at a time, and working quickly, break the eggs into a saucer and slip into the water. Cook until the whites are firm and the yolks are glazed but still liquid, 3–4 minutes, or until done to your liking.

7. Using a wire skimmer or slotted spoon, carefully remove each egg, and blot the bottom by resting the skimmer or spoon briefly on paper towels. Place 1 egg in the middle of each bed of watercress. Spoon the mushrooms and some of their juices around the eggs and slide 2 bread slice halves under the watercress on opposite sides of each plate. Drizzle the remaining dressing over the eggs and serve.

SERVES 4

NUTRITIONAL ANALYSIS PER SERVING
Calories 440 (Kilojoules 1,848); Protein 15 g; Carbohydrates 35 g; Total Fat 28 g;
Saturated Fat 5 g; Cholesterol 213 mg; Sodium 706 mg; Dietary Fiber 5 g

Potato Crisps with Northwest Caviar

¾ lb (375 g) Yukon gold or russet potatoes, peeled and very thinly sliced

2 tablespoons olive oil

½ teaspoon fine salt

¾ cup (6 fl oz/180 ml) crème fraîche or sour cream

3½ oz (105 g) ikura or other salted salmon roe

8 large fresh basil leaves, finely shredded

Chum salmon, the least popular salmon variety, produces the most sought-after ikura, or salted salmon roe. The lovely orange eggs make an affordable caviar. Prepare these crisps ahead of time and top them at the last minute. To slice the potatoes quickly and uniformly, use a mandoline.

1. Preheat the oven to 450°F (230°C).

2. Spread out the potato slices on 2 nonstick baking sheets and brush both sides with the olive oil. Do not overlap the slices. Sprinkle evenly with the salt.

3. Bake the potato slices until crisp, browned, and tender, 15–20 minutes. Remove from the oven and let cool completely.

4. To serve, top each potato slice with a dollop of crème fraîche or sour cream (about 1 teaspoon) and a bit of caviar (about ¼ teaspoon). Sprinkle the basil over the tops and arrange on a platter. Serve immediately.

MAKES ABOUT 40 CRISPS; SERVES 6

NUTRITIONAL ANALYSIS PER SERVING
Calories 197 (Kilojoules 827); Protein 6 g; Carbohydrates 11 g; Total Fat 15 g; Saturated Fat 5 g; Cholesterol 114 mg; Sodium 458 mg; Dietary Fiber 1 g

Oregon Blue Cheese Crackers

1 cup (5 oz/155 g) all-purpose (plain) flour

½ teaspoon fine salt

½ teaspoon freshly ground pepper

¼ cup (2 oz/60 g) chilled unsalted butter, cut up

¼ lb (125 g) Oregon blue or other blue cheese, crumbled

1 tablespoon chopped fresh sage

2 tablespoons water

Serve these crisp crackers, made with richly veined Oregon blue cheese, with a fine Northwest port and ripe pear slices for a satisfying snack or dessert.

1. In a large bowl, combine the flour, salt, and pepper and mix well. Using a pastry blender or 2 knives, mix in the butter, cheese, and sage until coarse crumbs form. Add the water and mix just until the dough comes together.

2. Preheat the oven to 350°F (180°C). Line 2 baking sheets with parchment (baking) paper.

3. Transfer the dough to a lightly floured work surface and roll out a sheet ⅛ inch (3 mm) thick. Using a fluted pastry wheel, cut out rectangular crackers measuring 1 by 1½ inches (2.5 by 4 cm). Transfer the crackers to the parchment-lined baking sheets.

4. Prick the middle of each cracker with a fork and bake until lightly browned, about 20 minutes. Using a spatula, transfer the crackers to a wire rack and let cool completely before serving. The crackers can be stored in an airtight container at room temperature for up to 1 week.

MAKES ABOUT 55 CRACKERS

NUTRITIONAL ANALYSIS PER CRACKER
Calories 25 (Kilojoules 105); Protein 1 g; Carbohydrates 2 g; Total Fat 1 g; Saturated Fat 1 g; Cholesterol 4 mg; Sodium 50 mg; Dietary Fiber 0 g

Peppered Salmon Trout and Plum Salad

The large Japanese-American population of the Northwest has introduced many Japanese ingredients into the local cuisine. Umeboshi plum vinegar, used in this salad, can be found in Asian markets and health-food stores. It is flavored with shiso leaves, pickled ume plums, and salt.

1. In a small bowl, whisk together the canola oil, vinegar, honey, and sesame oil to make a vinaigrette. Set aside.

2. In a small, dry frying pan over high heat, toast the sesame seeds, stirring frequently, until lightly browned, about 3 minutes. Transfer to a small bowl and let cool.

3. In a mixing bowl, combine the salad greens and the daikon or radishes. Drizzle with 2 tablespoons of the vinaigrette and toss well. Divide among individual plates. Transfer the plum slices to the same bowl, drizzle with 1 tablespoon of the vinaigrette, and toss well. Place the plums on top of the greens, dividing evenly.

4. Break the fish into 1½-inch (4-cm) chunks and arrange on top of the plums. Drizzle the salads with the remaining vinaigrette and sprinkle with the toasted sesame seeds. Serve immediately.

SERVES 4

NUTRITIONAL ANALYSIS PER SERVING
Calories 215 (Kilojoules 903); Protein 9 g; Carbohydrates 13 g; Total Fat 15 g;
Saturated Fat 2 g; Cholesterol 7 mg; Sodium 384 mg; Dietary Fiber 2 g

3 tablespoons canola oil

1 tablespoon umeboshi plum vinegar

1½ teaspoons honey

1 teaspoon Asian sesame oil

1 teaspoon sesame seeds

6 cups (18 oz/560 g) mixed baby salad greens

3-oz (90-g) piece daikon, peeled and finely julienned, or 1 cup (3 oz/90 g) finely julienned radishes

2 ripe black or red plums, pitted and cut into slices ¼ inch (6 mm) thick

¼ lb (125 g) peppered smoked salmon trout fillet or other smoked fish fillet

Spicy Cumin Walnuts

1 egg white

¼ cup (2 oz/60 g) firmly packed
  light brown sugar

1 tablespoon grated orange zest

1 teaspoon coarse salt

¾ teaspoon ground cumin

¼ teaspoon cayenne pepper

1 lb (500 g) walnut halves

I tasted my first freshly picked walnuts a couple of years ago at a mom-and-pop orchard outside of Anacortes, Washington. The outer hulls had already been removed and the nuts had been spread out to dry on wire racks for several days. The nuts were moist, buttery, and nearly addictive.

1. Preheat the oven to 350°F (180°C).

2. In a large bowl, whisk the egg white until foamy. Add the brown sugar, orange zest, salt, cumin, and cayenne and mix well. Add the nuts and toss to coat with the sugar mixture. Spread the nuts in a single layer on a large baking sheet or jelly-roll pan.

3. Bake the nuts for 12 minutes. Continue to bake, stirring frequently, until nicely browned, about 15 minutes longer. Remove from the oven and let cool completely on the pan before serving. The cooled nuts can also be stored in an airtight container at room temperature for several days or in the freezer for up to 3 months.

MAKES ABOUT 4 CUPS (1 LB/500 G)

NUTRITIONAL ANALYSIS PER ¼-CUP (1-OZ/30-G) SERVING
Calories 197 (Kilojoules 827); Protein 4 g; Carbohydrates 9 g; Total Fat 18 g;
Saturated Fat 2 g; Cholesterol 0 mg; Sodium 100 mg; Dietary Fiber 1 g

Wild Fennel Gravlax

1 teaspoon fennel seeds

¼ cup (2 oz/60 g) sugar

¼ cup (2 oz/60 g) coarse salt

1 teaspoon coarsely ground pepper

2 pieces salmon fillet, each about
½ lb (250 g)

1 cup (1½ oz/45 g) coarsely chopped
fronds and stems from common or
Florence (bulb) fennel

1 tablespoon vodka or aquavit

½ cup (4 oz/125 g) unsalted butter,
at room temperature

24 thin slices brown bread

6 lemon slices

In Seattle, wild fennel usually occupies any space forfeited by blackberry bushes. This fennel is known as common fennel (a different variety than Florence, or bulb, fennel), and its fronds are bushy and flavorful. It makes a nice change from the ubiquitous dill that usually flavors this dish. To ensure that the salmon is safe to eat raw, freeze it for 24 hours, then thaw in the refrigerator before using.

1. In a spice grinder or a mortar, coarsely grind the fennel seeds. Pour into a small bowl and add the sugar, salt, and pepper. Stir well.

2. Rub the salmon pieces on both sides with the fennel-seed mixture. Place 1 piece of salmon, flesh side up, on a plate and top with the fennel fronds. Sprinkle with the vodka or aquavit. Top with the second salmon fillet, flesh side down. Wrap the sandwiched fillets in plastic wrap. Place on a clean plate and top with a second plate. Place a 2–3-lb (1–1.5-kg) weight on top (several large cans work well). Refrigerate until the fish is somewhat opaque, about 24 hours.

3. To serve, scrape off the fennel fronds and other seasonings and pat the fish dry. Butter the bread slices. Slice the salmon against the grain about ⅛ inch (3 mm) thick and place on a platter with the lemon slices and buttered bread. Serve immediately.

SERVES 6

NUTRITIONAL ANALYSIS PER SERVING
Calories 432 (Kilojoules 1,814); Protein 20 g; Carbohydrates 31 g; Total Fat 25 g;
Saturated Fat 11 g; Cholesterol 86 mg; Sodium 1,655 mg; Dietary Fiber 3 g

Red Lentil Soup with Walla Walla Marmalade

1 cup (7 oz/220 g) red lentils

6 cups (48 fl oz/1.5 l) chicken or vegetable stock

1 bay leaf

salt to taste, plus ¼ teaspoon salt

¾ teaspoon freshly ground pepper

3 tablespoons unsalted butter

2 large Walla Walla or other sweet onions, about 1½ lb (750 g) total weight, chopped

1 teaspoon sugar

2 teaspoons chopped fresh thyme, plus whole leaves for garnish (optional)

1 teaspoon sherry vinegar

Walla Walla onions, which grow in the southeast corner of Washington State, are moist and sweet and have a short shelf life. Although at their best if eaten soon after purchase, they do store fairly well if hung in a sack in a cool, dark cellar or individually wrapped and slipped into the vegetable bin of a refrigerator.

1. Pick over the lentils and discard any misshapen ones or any stones. Rinse well.

2. In a large saucepan, combine the lentils, stock, and bay leaf and bring to a boil over high heat. Reduce the heat to a simmer and cook the lentils, uncovered, until they are very soft, 25–30 minutes. Remove from the heat and remove and discard the bay leaf.

3. Using an immersion blender, purée the soup until smooth. Alternatively, scoop out the lentils in 2 or 3 batches with a slotted spoon, place in a blender or food processor, and purée until smooth, adding a little of the cooking liquid if necessary. Return the purée to the pan. Season with salt and ½ teaspoon of the pepper.

4. While the lentils are cooking, in a frying pan over medium-high heat, melt the butter. Add the onions, sugar, and 2 teaspoons chopped thyme and cook, stirring often, until very soft and caramelized, about 25 minutes. Stir in the vinegar and season with the ¼ teaspoon salt and the remaining ¼ teaspoon pepper.

5. Ladle the soup into warmed bowls. Top each serving with the warm onion marmalade, dividing it evenly. If desired, garnish each serving with a few thyme leaves. Serve immediately.

SERVES 6

NUTRITIONAL ANALYSIS PER SERVING
Calories 202 (Kilojoules 848); Protein 13 g; Carbohydrates 24 g; Total Fat 6 g; Saturated Fat 4 g; Cholesterol 16 mg; Sodium 584 mg; Dietary Fiber 4 g

L ocated in the rain shadow of the Cascade Mountains is the Palouse. A variation of the French *pelouse,* meaning "lawn," this swath of rolling hills stretches across eastern Washington and Oregon and northern Idaho. Its potent combination of rich volcanic soil and summers of warm, dry days and cold nights makes it the ideal place for growing legumes for drying, such as chickpeas (garbanzo beans), green and yellow split peas, and the famous Palouse lentils.

In the early 1900s, legumes, both beans and peas, usually were grown as secondary crops in the Palouse. These plants helped to fertilize the soil with nitrogen for the more high-profile yields, such as wheat and barley. Eventually, legumes grew to become the region's number-one crop, and today 95 percent of the national dry pea and 98 percent of the national lentil crop are produced here.

Not long ago, most of the lentils cultivated in the Palouse were the familiar U.S. Regular, a large, brownish green lentil. But today, the Spanish Brown, or Pardina, lentil, a smaller, nutty-flavored variety, has become a regional favorite.

Palouse **Lentils**

Although lentils can be found in most markets, a wonderful mail-order source for specialty varieties is Zursun, started in the late 1980s in Twin Falls, Idaho. From her outpost in southern Idaho, Zursun's Lola Weyman ships Petite Crimson, Petite French Green, Red Chief, Beluga, and Pardina lentils, all grown in the Palouse.

Mussels in Thai Coconut Broth

2 lb (1 kg) mussels, well scrubbed
and debearded

½ cup (4 fl oz/125 ml) dry white wine

1 tablespoon canola oil

2 heads baby bok choy, trimmed and
cut into 1-inch (2.5-cm) pieces

1 red bell pepper (capsicum), seeded
and finely julienned

2 shallots, thinly sliced

2 teaspoons light brown sugar

1 teaspoon curry powder

large pinch of cayenne pepper

1 can (13 fl oz/430 ml) unsweetened
coconut milk, well shaken

¼ cup (¼ oz/7 g) fresh cilantro
(fresh coriander) leaves

4 lime wedges

The Northwest is famous for its farmed mussels, most of which come from areas in Puget Sound. Two types are grown: the Mediterranean mussel and the more dominant Penn Cove mussel. Since the two varieties have alternate spawning seasons, mussels are now available year-round. Store mussels for no more than a day after purchase, covered with a damp kitchen towel in your refrigerator, then scrub and debeard them just before cooking.

1. Place the mussels in a large saucepan, discarding any that fail to close to the touch. Add the wine and bring to a boil over high heat. Cover and cook, shaking the pan occasionally, until the mussels open, about 5 minutes. Using a slotted spoon, transfer the mussels to a bowl, discarding any that failed to open; cover and keep warm. Pour the liquid in the pan through a fine-mesh sieve lined with cheesecloth (muslin) and set aside.

2. Wipe out the pan, add the canola oil to it, and place over medium-high heat. When the oil is hot, add the bok choy, bell pepper, and shallots and cook, stirring, until the vegetables are soft, about 5 minutes. Stir in the brown sugar, curry powder, and cayenne. Pour in the coconut milk and the reserved mussel cooking liquid and bring to a boil over high heat.

3. Divide the mussels among warmed bowls and ladle the broth over the top, dividing evenly. Sprinkle with the cilantro and serve immediately with the lime wedges on the side.

SERVES 4

NUTRITIONAL ANALYSIS PER SERVING
Calories 313 (Kilojoules 1,315); Protein 11 g; Carbohydrates 11 g; Total Fat 25 g;
Saturated Fat 18 g; Cholesterol 18 mg; Sodium 223 mg; Dietary Fiber 1 g

2 Seafood, Poultry & Meats

The Pacific Northwest offers a stunning variety of fish and shellfish. From giant halibut to diminutive oysters, strange-looking geoducks to delicate singing scallops, blue-black mussels to myriad types of salmon, the choices are great, the flavors dazzling. The Northwest is also a wonderful resource for meats. Local organically raised poultry, lamb, and beef are readily available in many supermarkets. These high-quality meats make dishes such as Pork Chops with Apples and Cranberries (page 54) and Lamb Shanks with Merlot and Garlic (page 61) that much better. The region's spectacular vegetables (see recipes in Chapter 3) perfectly complement any of these dishes.

Grilled Spot Prawns

1½ lb (750 g) fresh or frozen spot
    prawns in the shell

3 tablespoons extra-virgin olive oil

2 tablespoons chopped fresh flat-leaf
    (Italian) parsley

1 teaspoon coarsely ground pepper

1 teaspoon coarse salt

grated zest of 2 lemons

Spot prawns are sweet shrimp that live in the waters off the coasts of Alaska, Washington, and Oregon. The females often come with the orange roe attached, an added treat. Here, the prawns are grilled with their shells on. Make sure the grill is very hot, so the fire can burnish the shells and give them a nice smoky flavor.

1. Prepare a hot fire in a charcoal grill, or preheat a gas or electric grill.

2. In a large bowl, combine the prawns, olive oil, parsley, pepper, salt, and lemon zest. Mix well to coat the prawns evenly with the other ingredients.

3. When the grill is very hot, place the prawns on the grill rack and grill, turning once, until they turn opaque and are just cooked through, 1–2 minutes on each side. Transfer to a platter and serve immediately.

SERVES 4

NUTRITIONAL ANALYSIS PER SERVING
Calories 96 (Kilojoules 403); Protein 10 g; Carbohydrates 1 g; Total Fat 6 g;
Saturated Fat 1 g; Cholesterol 70 mg; Sodium 253 mg; Dietary Fiber 0 g

Lamb with Balsamic Vinegar and Onions

2 tablespoons extra-virgin olive oil

2 Walla Walla or other sweet onions, thinly sliced

3 cloves garlic, minced

2 teaspoons chopped fresh rosemary

1 teaspoon sugar

¾ teaspoon coarse salt

¾ teaspoon freshly ground pepper

2 tablespoons olive oil

4 sirloin lamb chops, each about ½ lb (250 g) and 1 inch (2.5 cm) thick

½ cup (4 fl oz/125 ml) balsamic vinegar

Sirloin chops are cut from the upper part of the lamb leg. Although they are not as tender as loin or rib chops, they are very flavorful. The onions caramelize and become sweet in cooking. Serve a salad with plenty of bitter greens to act as a counterpoint.

1. In a large frying pan over medium heat, warm the extra-virgin olive oil. Add the onions, garlic, rosemary, and sugar and cook, stirring frequently, until the onions are soft and caramelized, about 25 minutes. Season with ¼ teaspoon each of the salt and pepper and transfer to a platter. Cover and keep warm.

2. Wipe out the pan, then add the olive oil and place over medium-high heat. Sprinkle the chops on both sides with the remaining ½ teaspoon each salt and pepper and add to the pan. Cook, turning once, until nicely browned on the outside and medium-rare at the center, 3–4 minutes on each side, or until done to your liking. Transfer the chops to the platter holding the onions.

3. Discard the fat from the frying pan and pour in the vinegar. Bring to a boil over high heat and deglaze the pan, stirring to scrape up any browned bits on the pan bottom. Cook until the liquid is reduced by half and syrupy, about 3 minutes.

4. Pour the reduced vinegar over the chops and serve immediately.

SERVES 4

NUTRITIONAL ANALYSIS PER SERVING
Calories 551 (Kilojoules 2,314); Protein 34 g; Carbohydrates 11 g; Total Fat 41 g; Saturated Fat 13 g; Cholesterol 128 mg; Sodium 377 mg; Dietary Fiber 2 g

Pacific
Salmon

Arriving at the confluence of the Columbia and Snake Rivers in 1805, explorers Meriwether Lewis and William Clark were amazed by the abundance of large salmon visible in the waters. For generations, Northwest Native Americans had virtually depended on the rivers for much of their food. Back then, it was said that a man could catch a full ton (1,000 kg) of fish in one day. But those times are long gone. Decimated by a host of evils, including overfishing, river dams, and a population boom, Pacific salmon are, today, in grave danger of extinction.

Pacific salmon are anadromous fish, meaning that they hatch in freshwater and migrate to saltwater. Five species, all belonging to the genus *Oncorhynchus,* or "hooked nose," are native to the Northwest.

Chinook, the most prized of the wild salmon, is famous for both its size and its flavor. Also called king or spring salmon, it typically weighs between six and twenty-five pounds (3 and 12 kg). It is the fattiest of all the species, which accounts for its rich taste.

Sockeye, also known as red salmon, is admired for its flavorful red meat and firm texture, and is the most sought-after variety in Japan. It averages about six pounds (3 kg).

The silver, or coho, is slightly larger than the sockeye but has a lower oil content and a lighter taste. Chum, or dog salmon, usually weighs eight to ten pounds (4 to 5 kg) and is one of the least expensive salmon.

The pink, or humpback, is quite small, commonly three to five pounds (1.5 to 2.5 kg). The most inexpensive of the five species, it is generally canned, although fresh pinks are sometimes found in ethnic markets.

Today, salmon remain an important part both of Northwest culture and of its cuisine, serving as the main attraction at countless community salmon roasts or barbecues. Native Americans continue their age-old tradition of smoke-roasting salmon. Threaded onto long split branches, with cedar twigs interwoven horizontally to keep the fish flat, whole sides of fish are slowly cooked over smoldering fires. Salmon is ever-present in homes as well as restaurants, whether it's green tea–baked salmon in banana leaves, a Cajun spice–rubbed fillet, a whole poached fish with fennel, or even salmon roe sushi.

A constant supply of salmon is available at markets today because of the abundance of farmed fish. Wild salmon possess more flavor variation than farmed, however, and the wild fish are in steady decline. Hoping to restore the native stock, the Endangered Species Act of March 1999 banned fishing for runs of wild Chinook, coho, chum, and sockeye in areas of Washington, Oregon, and Northern California. At stake is the very future of the wild Pacific salmon.

Infuse salmon with the flavors of lemon and herbs by stuffing them into the center cavity of a whole fish before cooking (opposite). Alder-smoked salmon, gravlax, and ikura, or salted roe (below), are Northwest specialties.

n with Pinot Noir and Thyme

A burgundy wine sauce looks beautiful drizzled over lustrous pink salmon. It is a simple reduction sauce, so you need to buy a good-quality Oregon Pinot Noir, some of the best of which come from the Willamette Valley. Remember, the better the wine, the better the sauce. Pour the rest of the bottle to accompany your dinner.

4 fresh thyme sprigs, plus extra for garnish (optional)

1 tablespoon unsalted butter

1. Sprinkle the salmon fillets with ½ teaspoon each of the salt and pepper.

2. In a large frying pan over high heat, warm the olive oil. Add the salmon, skin side down, and cook until browned and crisp, 3–4 minutes. Turn the fish and cook for 2–3 minutes longer. The salmon will be slightly rare at the center. If you prefer it fully cooked, continue cooking for another minute or so. Transfer the fish to a warmed platter and cover to keep warm.

3. Add the wine and the thyme sprigs to the pan and bring to a boil over high heat. Cook until reduced by half, about 5 minutes. Remove the thyme sprigs and stir in the remaining ¼ teaspoon each salt and pepper and the butter.

4. Pour the sauce over the salmon. Garnish with additional thyme sprigs, if you like, and serve immediately.

SERVES 4

NUTRITIONAL ANALYSIS PER SERVING
Calories 269 (Kilojoules 1,130); Protein 23 g; Carbohydrates 1 g; Total Fat 19 g; Saturated Fat 5 g; Cholesterol 75 mg; Sodium 346 mg; Dietary Fiber 0 g

Fried Oyster Sandwiches

COLESLAW

1 large head savoy cabbage, about
   1½ lb (750 g), cored and finely
   shredded

1½ tablespoons coarse salt

½ cup (4 fl oz/125 ml) buttermilk

2 tablespoons mayonnaise

2 tablespoons cider vinegar

1 teaspoon sugar

1 tablespoon chopped fresh dill

2 tablespoons chopped fresh flat-leaf
   (Italian) parsley

½ teaspoon freshly ground pepper

BATTER

1 cup (5 oz/155 g) all-purpose (plain)
   flour

¼ cup (1 oz/30 g) cornstarch
   (cornflour)

1 cup (8 fl oz/250 ml) pale ale

1 cup (5 oz/155 g) cornmeal

24 small oysters, in the shell, or 2 jars
   (10 oz/315 g each) shucked oysters

canola oil for frying

½ teaspoon coarse salt

½ teaspoon freshly ground pepper

4 crusty artisan rolls or pieces of
   baguette, split

4 lemon wedges

Add some oven fries to these succulent shellfish sandwiches, and a picnic in the backyard passes for a day at the beach.

1. To make the coleslaw, place the cabbage in a bowl and sprinkle with the salt. Toss and let stand until wilted, about 15 minutes. In a small bowl, stir together the buttermilk, mayonnaise, vinegar, sugar, dill, parsley, and pepper. Pour over the cabbage, toss well, and set aside.

2. If using oysters in the shell, working with 1 oyster at a time, and holding it over a bowl to capture the liquor (liquid), grip each shell, flat side up, with a folded kitchen towel. Push the tip of an oyster knife to one side of the hinge and pry upward to open the shell. Keeping the blade edge against the inside of the top shell, run the knife all around the oyster to sever the muscle that holds the shell halves together. Lift off and discard the top shell. Run the knife underneath the oyster to cut its flesh free from the bottom shell and set the oyster aside, discarding the shell. Repeat with the remaining oysters. Cover and refrigerate until needed.

3. To make the batter, in a small bowl, stir together the flour, cornstarch, and ale. Spread the cornmeal in a pie dish.

4. In a large, heavy frying pan over medium-high heat, pour in canola oil to a depth of ½ inch (12 mm). When the oil is hot, dip 4 or 5 oysters into the batter, then lift them out, letting the excess batter drip off. Turn the oysters in the cornmeal, coating evenly, and add to the oil. Fry, turning once, until golden brown, about 30 seconds on each side. Using a slotted spatula or tongs, transfer to paper towels to drain. Repeat with the remaining oysters. Sprinkle the fried oysters with the salt and pepper.

5. Place the roll bottoms on individual plates and top with the slaw. Top the slaw with 6 oysters per sandwich, and then with the roll tops. Garnish the plates with lemon wedges and serve.

SERVES 4

NUTRITIONAL ANALYSIS PER SERVING
Calories 623 (Kilojoules 2,617); Protein 20 g; Carbohydrates 85 g; Total Fat 24 g;
Saturated Fat 3 g; Cholesterol 36 mg; Sodium 2,361 mg; Dietary Fiber 3 g

Pork Chops with Apples and Cranberries

4 tablespoons (2 oz/60 g) unsalted butter

2 shallots, thinly sliced

2 tart green apples such as Newtown Pippin or Granny Smith, peeled, halved, cored, and cut lengthwise into slices ¼ inch (6 mm) thick

½ cup (2 oz/60 g) fresh or frozen cranberries

4 loin pork chops, each about ½ lb (250 g) and 1 inch (2.5 cm) thick

½ teaspoon coarse salt

½ teaspoon freshly ground pepper

¾ cup (6 fl oz/180 ml) hard cider or apple juice

½ teaspoon chopped fresh sage

Cranberries are commercially raised along the Oregon and Washington coasts, in areas where wild cranberries once flourished. If fresh or frozen berries aren't available for this dish, substitute dried cranberries, adding them to the sauce as it is reducing.

1. In a large frying pan over high heat, melt 2 tablespoons of the butter. Add the shallots and apples and cook, stirring frequently, until the apples are browned and slightly softened, about 5 minutes. Stir in the cranberries and cook until warmed through, about 1 minute longer. Transfer to a platter and keep warm.

2. Add 1 tablespoon of the remaining butter to the same pan over medium-high heat. Sprinkle the chops on both sides with the salt and pepper and add to the pan. Brown on the first side for 1 minute, then turn and brown on the second side for 1 minute. Cover and reduce the heat to low. Cook for 2 minutes, then turn the chops over and cook until done at the center but still pale pink, about 2 minutes longer. Transfer the chops to a platter, cover, and keep warm.

3. Return the apple mixture to the pan and add the cider or juice and the sage. Bring to a boil over high heat and deglaze the pan, stirring to scrape up any browned bits on the pan bottom. Cook until the liquid is reduced by half, 2–3 minutes, then swirl in the remaining 1 tablespoon butter.

4. Pour the sauce over the chops and serve immediately.

SERVES 4

NUTRITIONAL ANALYSIS PER SERVING
Calories 521 (Kilojoules 2,188); Protein 35 g; Carbohydrates 18 g; Total Fat 34 g; Saturated Fat 15 g; Cholesterol 143 mg; Sodium 275 mg; Dietary Fiber 2 g

For many years, my husband and I gathered at a friend's house for an annual apple tasting. Boisterously debating the merits of each apple, we sampled many varieties, from the Cox's Orange Pippin to the Liberty and Mutsu. Every year, our hands-down favorite was a Dutch apple with an operatic name and a brilliant flavor: the Karmijn de Sonnaville.

Washington's apple industry got its start in 1826, from seeds planted at Fort Vancouver, Washington. Today, more than half of the nation's eating apples come from orchards planted in the eastern foothills of the Cascade Mountains. Red and Golden Delicious apples predominate, but growers are expanding to include Galas, Braeburns, Gravensteins, and tart Granny Smiths and Newtown Pippins. Starring in both sweet and savory dishes, they also partner perfectly with Oregon blue or cheddar cheeses.

Not surprisingly, pears flourish in the Northwest as well, growing in the Medford and mid-Columbian regions of Oregon and the Yakima and Wenatchee Valleys of Washington. The crop includes the Bartlett (Williams') and Red Bartlett, Anjou

Apples and **Pears**

and Red Anjou, Bosc, Comice, and the smaller Seckel and Forelle.

Of course, pears are delightful both fresh and cooked. Crushed and distilled, however, they become a magnificent brandy or eau-de-vie. Clear Creek Distillery of Portland, Oregon, makes a lovely pear eau-de-vie, with a whole Hood River Bartlett floating inside each graceful bottle.

Manila Clams with Basil and Chiles

2 tablespoons canola oil

3 cloves garlic, coarsely chopped

1 Thai, jalapeño, or serrano chile, seeded and cut into long, narrow strips

1 red bell pepper (capsicum), seeded and cut into long, narrow strips

1 yellow bell pepper (capsicum), seeded and cut into long narrow strips

3 lb (1.5 kg) Manila or littleneck clams, scrubbed

1 tablespoon Thai roasted chile paste

1 tablespoon fish sauce

½ cup (½ oz/15 g) fresh horapah basil or other basil leaves, torn if large

¼ cup (¼ oz/7 g) fresh mint leaves

Both Thai and Vietnamese cuisines use healthy amounts of horapah basil, an aromatic plant with purple stems and shiny leaves. Most Asian markets carry it, but you may substitute the more common Italian, or sweet, basil, if necessary. Serve these fiery clams with plenty of steamed jasmine rice and a Northwest ale.

1. Place a large, deep frying pan or wok over high heat. When the pan is hot, add the canola oil and swirl to coat the bottom of the pan. When the oil is hot but not smoking, add the garlic. Cook, stirring, until golden, about 30 seconds. Add the chile pepper and the red and yellow bell peppers and cook, stirring constantly, until lightly cooked, 1–2 minutes.

2. Add the clams, discarding any that fail to close to the touch. Stir to coat with the oil. Cook, tossing and stirring, for 2 minutes, then stir in the chile paste and the fish sauce. Cook, stirring frequently, until the clams have opened, 3–5 minutes longer. Stir in the basil and mint.

3. Transfer the clams to a platter or serving bowl, discarding any that failed to open. Serve immediately.

SERVES 4

NUTRITIONAL ANALYSIS PER SERVING
Calories 111 (Kilojoules 525); Protein 8 g; Carbohydrates 6 g; Total Fat 8 g;
Saturated Fat 1 g; Cholesterol 17 mg; Sodium 352 mg; Dietary Fiber 1 g

Oregon Peppered Bacon and Crab BLT

1 red bell pepper (capsicum)

½ cup (4 fl oz/125 ml) mayonnaise

1 tablespoon chopped fresh tarragon

4 thick slices peppered bacon, about 6 oz (185 g) total weight

4 crusty artisan bread rolls, split and lightly toasted

1½ cups (8 oz/250 g) fresh-cooked Dungeness crabmeat, picked over for shell fragments

2 ripe tomatoes, sliced ¼ inch (6 mm) thick

1 small head butter (Boston) or Bibb lettuce, leaves separated

This is not your average BLT. The Northwest's popular peppered bacon joins Dungeness crab and tarragon to deliver delightful—and unexpected—flavors to this classic sandwich. For a special-occasion lunch, prepare all the elements ahead of time, then assemble the sandwiches just before serving.

1. Preheat the broiler (griller). Cut the bell pepper in half lengthwise and remove the stem, seeds, and ribs. Place, cut sides down, on a baking sheet. Broil (grill) until the skin blackens and blisters. Remove from the broiler, drape loosely with aluminum foil, and let cool for 10 minutes, then peel away the skin. Chop finely and place in a small bowl. Add the mayonnaise and tarragon and mix well.

2. Meanwhile, in a large frying pan over medium-high heat, fry the bacon until crisp, about 10 minutes. Using tongs, transfer to paper towels to drain.

3. Spread the cut surfaces of the rolls with the mayonnaise mixture, dividing it evenly between the tops and bottoms.

4. Place the bottoms of the rolls on individual plates and top with the crabmeat, tomatoes, bacon, and lettuce. Cover with the roll tops and secure each sandwich with 2 toothpicks. Cut each sandwich in half between the toothpicks and serve.

SERVES 4

NUTRITIONAL ANALYSIS PER SERVING
Calories 500 (Kilojoules 2,100); Protein 21 g; Carbohydrates 34 g; Total Fat 31 g; Saturated Fat 6 g; Cholesterol 83 mg; Sodium 843 mg; Dietary Fiber 3 g

Mashed Potato–Salmon Cakes

1½ lb (750 g) russet or Yukon gold potatoes, peeled and cut into 1-inch (2.5-cm) chunks

1¼ teaspoons salt

½ teaspoon freshly ground pepper

4 green (spring) onions, thinly sliced

¼ lb (125 g) alder-smoked kippered salmon fillet, broken into small chunks

¼ cup (1 oz/30 g) fine dried bread crumbs

2 tablespoons unsalted butter

2 tablespoons canola oil

2 cups (12 oz/375 g) yellow or red cherry tomatoes, or a mixture

¾ cup (6 fl oz/180 ml) sour cream

2 tablespoons prepared horseradish

These salmon cakes are made with alder-smoked kippered salmon, a specialty developed by Native Americans in the Pacific Northwest. Since most people don't have leftover mashed potatoes on hand, I've included instructions for how to make 2 cups (1 lb/500 g), the amount needed for the recipe.

1. Place the potatoes in a saucepan with water to cover by 1 inch (2.5 cm) and 1 teaspoon of the salt. Bring to a boil over high heat, reduce the heat to medium, and simmer, uncovered, until very tender, about 10 minutes. Drain and pass through a ricer or a food mill placed over a bowl; let cool. Stir in ¼ teaspoon of the pepper, the green onions, and the salmon.

2. Shape the mixture into 8 cakes, each 3 inches (7.5 cm) in diameter. Place on a plate, cover, and refrigerate until cold, about 1 hour.

3. Preheat the oven to 250°F (120°C).

4. Spread the bread crumbs on waxed paper or in a pie dish. Coat the cakes evenly with the bread crumbs, tapping off the excess. Set aside.

5. In a large frying pan over medium-high heat, warm 1 tablespoon each of the butter and the canola oil. Add half of the cakes and fry, turning once, until golden brown, 3–4 minutes on each side. Transfer the cakes to a heatproof platter and place in the oven. Add the remaining 1 tablespoon each butter and oil to the pan and repeat with the remaining cakes. Transfer to the oven.

6. Add the tomatoes and the remaining ¼ teaspoon salt and ¼ teaspoon pepper to the frying pan over high heat. Cook briefly, just until the tomatoes soften, 1–2 minutes. Remove from the heat. In a small bowl, stir together the sour cream and horseradish.

7. Serve the potato-salmon cakes with the tomatoes spooned on the side of the platter. Pass the sour cream sauce at the table.

SERVES 4

NUTRITIONAL ANALYSIS PER SERVING
Calories 414 (Kilojoules 1,739); Protein 12 g; Carbohydrates 40 g; Total Fat 24 g; Saturated Fat 10 g; Cholesterol 41 mg; Sodium 1,117 mg; Dietary Fiber 4 g

Lamb Shanks with Merlot and Garlic

Lamb shanks become tender and juicy when braised in a good Pacific Northwest Merlot. If your pot is smaller than 10 inches (25 cm) in diameter, ask your butcher to crack the bones so the shanks will fit. Serve with lots of fresh crusty bread to mop up the sauce.

1. Preheat the oven to 350°F (180°C).

2. Trim off any excess fat from the lamb shanks. Sprinkle the shanks with the salt and pepper. Spread the flour on a plate and turn the shanks in the flour, shaking off any excess.

3. In a large, heavy ovenproof pot over high heat, warm 2 tablespoons of the olive oil. Add the shanks (in batches, if necessary) and brown well on all sides, about 5 minutes. Transfer the shanks to a plate. Wipe out the pot.

4. Add the remaining 2 tablespoons oil to the pot over medium-high heat. Add the onion and cook, stirring frequently, until soft, 3–4 minutes. Return the shanks to the pot along with the potatoes, carrots, garlic, bay leaves, thyme, wine, and stock. Bring to a boil, cover, and transfer to the oven.

5. Bake for 1½ hours. Uncover and continue to bake until the lamb is very tender, about 30 minutes longer. Transfer the shanks to a platter. Using a slotted spoon, transfer the potatoes and carrots to the platter. Cover and keep warm.

6. Using a large spoon, skim off any fat from the surface of the sauce remaining in the pot. Lift out and discard the bay leaves and the thyme. Place the pot over high heat and bring to a boil. Cook the sauce until it reduces and is lightly thickened, 3–5 minutes.

7. Pour the sauce around the meat. Sprinkle the meat and vegetables with the parsley and mint.

SERVES 4

NUTRITIONAL ANALYSIS PER SERVING
Calories 691 (Kilojoules 2,902); Protein 61 g; Carbohydrates 54 g; Total Fat 26 g; Saturated Fat 6 g; Cholesterol 166 mg; Sodium 836 mg; Dietary Fiber 7 g

4 meaty lamb shanks, ¾–1 lb (375–500 g) each

1 teaspoon coarse salt

½ teaspoon freshly ground pepper

¼ cup (1½ oz/45 g) all-purpose (plain) flour

4 tablespoons (2 fl oz/60 ml) olive oil

1 large Walla Walla or other sweet onion, chopped

1 lb (500 g) Yukon gold or Yellow Finn potatoes, unpeeled, cut into 1½-inch (4-cm) chunks

1 lb (500 g) carrots, peeled, split lengthwise, and cut into 1-inch (2.5-cm) pieces

2 heads garlic, cloves separated and peeled

2 bay leaves

1 bunch fresh thyme, tied in a bundle

1 cup (8 fl oz/250 ml) Merlot

1 cup (8 fl oz/250 ml) chicken stock

2 tablespoons chopped fresh flat-leaf (Italian) parsley

1 tablespoon chopped fresh mint

Grilled Black Cod with Cucumbers and Ginger

2 English (hothouse) cucumbers, very
thinly sliced

1 cup (3½ oz/105 g) very thinly
sliced red (Spanish) onion

2 teaspoons coarse salt

3 tablespoons chopped pickled ginger

1 tablespoon unseasoned rice vinegar

3 tablespoons canola oil

4 black cod fillets, about 1½ lb
(750 g) total weight

½ teaspoon freshly ground pepper

Black cod, or sablefish, is a mild, buttery fish with a firm
texture. It is fished from Southern California to the Bering
Sea, from January through September. If unavailable,
Chilean sea bass or halibut would make a fine substitute.

1. Prepare a hot fire in a charcoal grill, or preheat a gas or electric grill.
Oil the grill rack.

2. In a bowl, combine the cucumbers and onion and sprinkle with
1½ teaspoons of the salt. Let stand for 15 minutes. Stir in the ginger,
vinegar, and 2 tablespoons of the canola oil. Set aside.

3. Brush the fish fillet on both sides with the remaining 1 tablespoon
oil. Sprinkle on both sides with the remaining ½ teaspoon salt and
the pepper.

4. Place the fish, skin side down, over the fire and grill, turning once,
until just opaque throughout, about 8 minutes total.

5. Transfer the cod fillets to warmed individual plates. Serve immediately with the cucumber salad.

SERVES 4

NUTRITIONAL ANALYSIS PER SERVING
Calories 290 (Kilojoules 1,218); Protein 33 g; Carbohydrates 13 g; Total Fat 11 g;
Saturated Fat 1 g; Cholesterol 73 mg; Sodium 881 mg; Dietary Fiber 3 g

Beer-Braised Short Ribs

2 tablespoons canola oil

3–4 lb (1.5–2 kg) beef short ribs, from chuck or rib sections, trimmed of excess fat

1 teaspoon coarse salt

1 teaspoon freshly ground pepper

¼ cup (1½ oz/45 g) all-purpose (plain) flour

2 leeks, white and pale green parts only, chopped

2 cloves garlic, minced

2 tablespoons peeled and chopped fresh ginger

1 tablespoon firmly packed light brown sugar

4 large parsnips, about 1¼ lb (625 g) total weight, peeled and cut into 1-inch (2.5-cm) lengths

8 carrots, peeled and cut into 1-inch (2.5-cm) lengths

2 bay leaves

1 bottle (12 fl oz/375 ml) Hefeweizen or brown ale

1 cup (8 fl oz/250 ml) beef stock

2 tablespoons chopped fresh flat-leaf (Italian) parsley

These ribs are braised in Hefeweizen, a cloudy unfiltered beer made from wheat malt by many microbreweries in the Pacific Northwest. The beer blends well with the fresh ginger and brown sugar that flavor the stew. Pour more Hefeweizen to drink at the table—slip a lemon wedge in each glass— and serve buttered caraway noodles on the side.

1. Preheat the oven to 350°F (180°C).

2. In a dutch oven or large, heavy, deep, ovenproof frying pan, warm the canola oil until very hot. Meanwhile, sprinkle the ribs with the salt and pepper. Spread the flour on a plate and turn the ribs in the flour, coating evenly and shaking off any excess. In batches, add the ribs to the hot oil and brown on all sides, 6–7 minutes for each batch. Transfer to a plate.

3. Pour off all but 2 tablespoons of the fat and return the dutch oven to medium-high heat. Add the leeks, garlic, ginger, and brown sugar and cook, stirring frequently, until the leeks are soft, 2–3 minutes. Stir in the parsnips, carrots, and bay leaves and return the meat to the dutch oven. Pour in the beer and beef stock, and bring to a boil over high heat. Cover, transfer to the oven, and bake until the ribs are very tender, about 2 hours.

4. Using a slotted spoon, transfer the meat and vegetables to a deep platter. Cover and keep warm. Using a large spoon, skim off any fat from the surface of the cooking liquid and discard the bay leaves. Bring to a boil over high heat and simmer until the liquid is slightly reduced, 3–4 minutes.

5. Spoon the sauce over the meat and vegetables, sprinkle with the parsley, and serve.

SERVES 6

NUTRITIONAL ANALYSIS PER SERVING
Calories 682 (Kilojoules 2,864); Protein 28 g; Carbohydrates 39 g; Total Fat 46 g; Saturated Fat 18 g; Cholesterol 106 mg; Sodium 520 mg; Dietary Fiber 8 g

Mustard-Grilled Halibut

¼ cup (2 oz/60 g) coarse-grain
mustard

3 tablespoons extra-virgin olive oil

4 halibut steaks, each about 6 oz
(185 g) and 1 inch (2.5 cm) thick

½ teaspoon coarse salt

½ teaspoon freshly ground pepper

2 teaspoons chopped fresh tarragon

When summer arrives in the Pacific Northwest, so does fresh halibut. Sold frozen the remainder of the year, Pacific halibut is a large, mild flatfish with firm, white flesh. Round out the menu with some grilled vegetables and potatoes and pour a Chardonnay.

1. Prepare a hot fire in a charcoal grill, or preheat a gas or electric grill.

2. In a small bowl, stir together the mustard and olive oil. Lightly brush most of the mixture on both sides of the fish and sprinkle with the salt and pepper.

3. Generously oil the grill rack. Place the halibut steaks on the rack and grill for about 4 minutes. Turn the steaks and brush with the remaining mustard mixture. Continue to grill just until the flesh starts to separate from the bone and is opaque throughout, 3–4 minutes longer.

4. Transfer the halibut steaks to individual plates and sprinkle with the tarragon. Serve immediately.

SERVES 4

NUTRITIONAL ANALYSIS PER SERVING
Calories 257 (Kilojoules 1,079); Protein 29 g; Carbohydrates 0 g; Total Fat 14 g;
Saturated Fat 2 g; Cholesterol 44 mg; Sodium 428 mg; Dietary Fiber 0 g

A ugust 17, 1907, was opening day at Seattle's Pike Place Market. With the chance to buy directly from local farmers, excited shoppers flooded the site. Although only a half-dozen overwhelmed purveyors were present, Pike Place became an immediate and unqualified success.

Today, the market is one of the country's oldest continuously operating farmers' markets. A nine-acre (3.6-hectare) historical district, it offers everything from produce, meats, poultry, and fish to kitchenware, crafts, and books.

On summer weekends, the market overflows with street musicians and tourists amid the vegetables and flowers. I prefer to go on Wednesdays (organic day) to buy slender haricots verts and ripe tomatoes. In fall, I am lured by the winter squashes, kale, and wild mushrooms. The winter is a bit quieter, but farmers still bring in lovely root vegetables such as potatoes, beets, and parsnips. Spring delivers peas and pea shoots, as well as young lettuces and Asian greens.

The market also offers some of the freshest fish around. My favorite purveyor, Pure Food Fish Market,

Pike Place Market

dates back to about 1917, making it one of the earliest fish stores still operating. The bountiful displays of salmon, spot prawns, oysters, and crabs can make decisions difficult.

Although the market has experienced tough times, today it is easily Seattle's most popular tourist attraction. Indeed, no visit to Seattle is complete without a trip to Pike Place.

Salt and Pepper Squid

2 lb (1 kg) squid

1 cup (5 oz/155 g) all-purpose (plain) flour

1 tablespoon coarse salt

1 teaspoon coarsely ground pepper

canola oil for deep-frying

lemon wedges

Squid is wonderfully light and crisp when treated to a dusting of flour and a brief dunking in very hot oil. Coarse salt and pepper and a crowning spritz of fresh lemon juice complete the dish.

1. To clean each squid, grip the head and pull it and the attached innards from the body. Squeeze out the small, hard beak at the base of the tentacles. Using a small, sharp knife, cut away the eyes; set the tentacles aside. Pull out the transparent quill-like cartilage from the body and discard, then, using a finger, clean out the body pouch, holding it under cold running water as you work. Rub off the mottled skin on the outside of the pouch. Rinse the pouch and tentacles well. Cut the bodies into rings ½ inch (12 mm) wide; leave the tentacles whole. If you are using already cleaned squid, simply cut the bodies into rings.

2. In a shallow bowl, stir together the flour, salt, and pepper.

3. Pour canola oil into a deep, heavy saucepan to a depth of 3 inches (7.5 cm) and heat to 375°F (190°C) on a deep-frying thermometer. When the oil is ready, add about one-third of the squid to the flour mixture, turn to coat evenly, and then shake off the excess. Add the squid to the oil, stir briefly, and cook for 1 minute. The squid should be opaque and perfectly tender. Using a wire skimmer, lift out the squid and place on paper towels to drain briefly. Repeat with the remaining squid in two batches.

4. Transfer the squid to a platter and serve immediately with lemon wedges.

SERVES 4

NUTRITIONAL ANALYSIS PER SERVING
Calories 271 (Kilojoules 1,138); Protein 25 g; Carbohydrates 13 g; Total Fat 12 g; Saturated Fat 1 g; Cholesterol 362 mg; Sodium 437 mg; Dietary Fiber 0 g

Five-Spice Duck Wraps

DIPPING SAUCE

3 cloves garlic, coarsely chopped

2 tablespoons sugar

½ teaspoon red pepper flakes

¼ cup (2 fl oz/60 ml) fresh lime juice

¼ cup (2 fl oz/60 ml) unseasoned
  rice vinegar

¼ cup (2 fl oz/60 ml) fish sauce

1 carrot, peeled and shredded

2 boneless whole duck breasts, about
  1¼ lb (625 g) total weight, split
  in half

½ teaspoon Chinese five-spice powder

½ teaspoon coarse salt

½ teaspoon freshly ground black
  pepper

8 whole-wheat (wholemeal) flour
  tortillas

1 tablespoon canola oil

1 bunch arugula (rocket), mizuna, or
  watercress, tough stems removed

½ cup (½ oz/15 g) fresh cilantro
  (fresh coriander) leaves

½ cup (½ oz/15 g) fresh mint leaves

½ cup (½ oz/15 g) fresh basil leaves

A blend of Asian and Latin flavors, these duck wraps exemplify Northwest fusion cooking. The duck and its seasonings are Asian inspired, while the wrap is a simple tortilla. I prefer whole-wheat tortillas, but you can use white-flour ones instead. If you wish, substitute chicken breasts for the duck.

1. To make the dipping sauce, in a bowl, stir together the garlic, sugar, red pepper flakes, lime juice, rice vinegar, and fish sauce until the sugar dissolves. Stir in the carrot and set aside.

2. Remove the skin from the duck breasts. Rub the duck breasts on both sides with the five-spice powder, salt, and black pepper. Set aside on a plate for 15 minutes at room temperature.

3. Preheat the oven to 450°F (230°C). Wrap the tortillas in aluminum foil and place in the oven until hot, about 8 minutes.

4. While the tortillas are heating, in a large ovenproof frying pan over medium-high heat, warm the canola oil. When the oil is hot, add the duck breasts and cook, turning once, until browned on both sides, about 3 minutes on each side. Transfer the pan to the oven and bake the breasts until they are medium-rare when cut into at the center, about 5 minutes. Remember to check the tortillas at this point and remove them if they are ready. Transfer the duck breasts to a cutting board, cover, and let rest for 5 minutes.

5. To serve, cut the breasts into thin slices against the grain and arrange attractively on a platter. Surround with the arugula or other greens and the cilantro, mint, and basil. Serve the tortillas and dipping sauce on the side. Each diner wraps the duck slices, greens, and herbs in a tortilla, as if making a burrito.

SERVES 4

NUTRITIONAL ANALYSIS PER SERVING
Calories 529 (Kilojoules 2,222); Protein 37 g; Carbohydrates 71 g; Total Fat 11 g;
Saturated Fat 2 g; Cholesterol 131 mg; Sodium 1,691 mg; Dietary Fiber 6 g

Blackberry-Barbecued Chicken

1 tablespoon canola oil

1 cup (4 oz/125 g) chopped Walla Walla or other sweet onion

½ cup (4 fl oz/125 ml) red wine

2 pt (1 lb/500 g) fresh or frozen blackberries

¼ cup (2 oz/60 g) firmly packed light brown sugar

1 teaspoon soy sauce

1 chicken, 3½ lb (1.75 kg), cut into 8 serving pieces

½ teaspoon coarse salt

½ teaspoon freshly ground pepper

This barbecue sauce recipe makes enough for two chickens. Store the leftover sauce in a tightly capped container in the refrigerator for several days or in the freezer for several months. Make a batch of Walla Walla Onion Rings (page 86) and a green bean salad to go alongside, and you'll be all set.

1. To make the barbecue sauce, in a large saucepan over medium-high heat, warm the canola oil. Add the onion and cook, stirring frequently, until soft, about 5 minutes. Add the wine, berries, brown sugar, and soy sauce and cook until slightly thickened, about 15 minutes. Remove from the heat and pass the sauce through a food mill placed over a bowl, or purée in a blender or food processor and pass through a fine-mesh sieve placed over a bowl. Set aside.

2. While the sauce is cooking, prepare a medium-hot fire in a charcoal grill, or preheat a gas or electric grill to medium-high. Oil the grill rack.

3. Sprinkle the chicken with the salt and pepper. Place the chicken pieces, skin side down, on the grill rack and cook for 5 minutes. Baste with the sauce and cook for 5 minutes longer. Turn the pieces, baste again, and cook until the juices run clear when a thigh is pierced, about 5 minutes longer. Some pieces will cook more quickly than others. The white-meat pieces, for example, should be moved to the outsides of the rack where the heat is less intense.

4. Transfer the chicken pieces to a platter and brush with additional sauce. Serve immediately.

SERVES 4

NUTRITIONAL ANALYSIS PER SERVING
Calories 576 (Kilojoules 2,419); Protein 49 g; Carbohydrates 32 g; Total Fat 28 g; Saturated Fat 7 g; Cholesterol 154 mg; Sodium 423 mg; Dietary Fiber 6 g

Cornmeal-Coated Trout with Fried Sage

Since most trout available in fish markets today is farmed, you can make this simple dish any time of year. If you prepare it in the spring, however, you will be able to clip fresh sage from your garden. Don't stint on the amount, because once the leaves are fried, they will be eaten up quickly.

1. Sprinkle the salt and pepper evenly over the trout. Spread the cornmeal on a large plate and coat the trout evenly with it. Set aside.

2. In a large frying pan over medium-high heat, melt 1 tablespoon of the butter. Add the pancetta and cook, stirring, until browned and crisp, 6–7 minutes. Using a slotted spoon, transfer to paper towels to drain.

3. Add 2 tablespoons of the olive oil to the pan and heat until almost smoking. Add the sage leaves and cook until they just begin to turn gray, 10–15 seconds. Using the slotted spoon, transfer the leaves to paper towels to drain. Drain off the oil from the pan into a small dish.

4. Wipe out the pan, then return the reserved oil to it. Add the remaining 1 tablespoon each butter and oil and place over medium-high heat. When hot, add the trout and cook, turning once, until golden brown and opaque throughout, 3–4 minutes on each side.

5. Transfer to a warmed platter or individual plates and sprinkle with the pancetta, sage leaves, and lemon zest. Serve immediately.

SERVES 4

NUTRITIONAL ANALYSIS PER SERVING
Calories 434 (Kilojoules 1,823); Protein 30 g; Carbohydrates 12 g; Total Fat 30 g;
Saturated Fat 9 g; Cholesterol 102 mg; Sodium 411 mg; Dietary Fiber 1 g

¾ teaspoon coarse salt

¾ teaspoon freshly ground pepper

4 rainbow trout, 6–8 oz (185–250 g) each, cleaned with heads and tails intact

⅓ cup (2 oz/60 g) coarsely ground cornmeal

2 tablespoons unsalted butter

2 slices pancetta, each about ¼ inch (6 mm) thick, diced

3 tablespoons extra-virgin olive oil

24 fresh sage leaves

2 teaspoons finely grated lemon zest

Chicken, Blue Cheese, and Arugula Salad

6 tablespoons (3 fl oz/90 ml) extra-virgin olive oil

2 teaspoons tarragon vinegar or white wine vinegar

2 teaspoons fresh lemon juice

¾ teaspoon coarse salt

¾ teaspoon freshly ground pepper

4 slices artisan walnut bread or other artisan bread, each about ½ inch (12 mm) thick

1 clove garlic, halved

4 boneless, skinless chicken breast halves, each about 5 oz (155 g)

2 large bunches arugula (rocket), tough stems removed

1 cup (5 oz/155 g) crumbled Oregon blue or other blue cheese

½ pt (4 oz/125 g) berries such as raspberries, marionberries, or blackberries

2 tablespoons chopped fresh tarragon

2 tablespoons chopped fresh basil

This casual main-dish salad exemplifies a favorite way to eat: everything—salad, meat, cheese, bread, berries—served on a single plate. To complete this perfect summer meal, pour a glass of chilled Washington State Riesling.

1. In a large bowl, whisk together 3 tablespoons of the olive oil, the vinegar, the lemon juice, and ¼ teaspoon each of the salt and pepper. Set aside.

2. Toast the bread slices in a toaster or in a preheated broiler (griller) until golden brown on both sides. Rub one side of each slice with the garlic and then brush with 1 tablespoon of the oil. Set aside.

3. In a large frying pan over medium-high heat, warm the remaining 2 tablespoons olive oil. Sprinkle the chicken with the remaining ½ teaspoon each salt and pepper and add to the hot oil. Cook, turning once, until the juices run clear when pierced at the thickest point, 10–12 minutes total. Remove from the heat and transfer to a cutting board.

4. Toss the arugula leaves with the dressing to coat. Divide the arugula among individual plates. Cut each chicken breast half into 3 or 4 lengthwise slices and fan out the slices on top of the arugula. Cut the toasted bread slices in half and place next to the chicken. Sprinkle the blue cheese, berries, tarragon, and basil over the top of the salads. Serve at once.

SERVES 4

NUTRITIONAL ANALYSIS PER SERVING
Calories 635 (Kilojoules 2,667); Protein 47 g; Carbohydrates 35 g; Total Fat 36 g; Saturated Fat 10 g; Cholesterol 109 mg; Sodium 1,178 mg; Dietary Fiber 5 g

Burgers with Smoked Gouda and Leeks

3 tablespoons unsalted butter

3 large leeks, white and pale green parts only, thinly sliced

1 tablespoon thinly sliced chives

1 teaspoon coarse salt

1 teaspoon freshly ground pepper

1¼ lb (625 g) ground (minced) beef, preferably chuck

4 thin slices smoked Gouda or other smoked cheese, each about 1 oz (30 g)

¼ cup (2 fl oz/60 ml) mayonnaise

1½ tablespoons Dijon mustard

4 crusty artisan rolls, split

1 small head butter (Boston) or Bibb lettuce, leaves separated

The Pacific Northwest abounds in small purveyors of high-quality products. The first time I made these burgers I used organic beef from a farm outside of Bellingham, Washington; leeks from a farmer on nearby Lopez Island; and smoked Gouda from a cheese maker in Oregon.

1. Prepare a hot fire in a charcoal grill with a cover, or preheat a gas or electric grill with a cover. Oil the grill rack.

2. In a large frying pan over medium-high heat, melt the butter. Add the leeks and cook, stirring frequently, until very soft, about 10 minutes. Stir in the chives and ½ teaspoon each of the salt and pepper. Transfer to a bowl, cover, and keep warm.

3. In a large bowl, combine the beef and the remaining ½ teaspoon each salt and pepper. Mix well and divide into 4 equal portions. Form each portion into a patty about 1 inch (2.5 cm) thick.

4. Place the patties on the grill rack and cook for about 4 minutes. Turn the patties and place a slice of cheese on each one. Cover the grill and cook for 4 minutes longer for medium-rare, or until done to your liking. (Subtract 1 minute on each side for rare, or add 1 minute on each side for well done.)

5. Meanwhile, in a small bowl, stir together the mayonnaise and mustard. Place the roll halves, cut sides up, on individual plates. Spread them with the mayonnaise mixture and top with the lettuce leaves, dividing evenly.

6. When the burgers are done, transfer them to the lettuce-topped roll bottoms and top with the leeks. Cover with the roll tops and serve immediately.

SERVES 4

NUTRITIONAL ANALYSIS PER SERVING
Calories 822 (Kilojoules 3,452); Protein 42 g; Carbohydrates 50 g; Total Fat 50 g; Saturated Fat 20 g; Cholesterol 164 mg; Sodium 1,333 mg; Dietary Fiber 3 g

M ost artisan loaves are European-style rustic breads with wonderful crusts and earthy flavors. As the 1980s' food revolution evolved, it was only natural for great bread to develop right along with it. Today, a good loaf of bread is as much a part of the Northwest table as a bottle of the superb local wine.

In the Northwest, several bakeries had long turned out French baguettes, but the first true artisan-bread bakery was Grand Central, which opened in 1989, in Seattle's Pioneer Square. Gwen Bassetti was the brains behind this innovative operation, and she continues to be a leading figure in the Northwest bread-baking world. In those early days, Gwen, along with head baker Leslie Mackie (now owner of Seattle's Macrina Bakery), produced five varieties of crusty, brown loaves from an Italian hearth oven. Within a month of the bakery's launch, people were lining up for their daily rations of crusty Como and eight-grain Campagnola.

As the demand for rustic breads grew, new bakeries sprang up across the Northwest. Some of the best artisan bakeries you'll find locally are Essential (specializing in organic

Artisan **Bread**

loaves) and La Panzanella of Seattle and Marsee and Pearl of Portland. With breads as varied as potato, olive, German-style Volkhorn, whole-wheat walnut, and crusty ciabatta, there's an artisan bread to suit every palate and every meal. Although bread has always been a staple here, now it also is one of the region's most exceptional products.

Lingcod en Papillote

2 tablespoons unsalted butter

½ cup (3 oz/90 g) minced red (Spanish) onion

1 lb (500 g) fresh wild mushrooms, such as chanterelle, morel, or porcini, or cultivated mushrooms, such as portobello or cremini, or a mixture, brushed clean and cut into ½-inch (12-mm) pieces

1½ teaspoons chopped fresh rosemary

4 lingcod fillets, each 5–6 oz (155–185 g) and ¾ inch (2 cm) thick

¾ teaspoon coarse salt

¾ teaspoon freshly ground pepper

1½ teaspoons grated lemon zest

2 tablespoons dry white wine

En papillote describes a simple, effective way to steam fish and vegetables together in a parchment (baking) paper or foil parcel. Here, lingcod, a large commercial catch from Washington State, is used. The flavors of the fish and vegetables intermingle, resulting in a juicy, ready-to-eat meal.

1. In a large frying pan over medium-high heat, melt the butter. Add the onion and cook, stirring frequently, until soft, 2–3 minutes. Add the mushrooms and cook, stirring occasionally, until tender, 5–7 minutes. Stir in the rosemary and remove from the heat.

2. Preheat the oven to 450°F (230°C).

3. Cut out four 14-inch (35-cm) squares of parchment (baking) paper or aluminum foil. Fold each square in half. Place a fish fillet on one-half of the folded square. Sprinkle the fillets evenly with the salt, pepper, and lemon zest and top evenly with the mushroom mixture. Sprinkle with the wine, again dividing evenly. Bring up the sides of the parchment or foil and fold over the edges to seal the fish securely in the packet. Place the packets on a baking sheet.

4. Bake the packets for 8 minutes. If the fish is the thickness specified, the fillets should be properly cooked. If you have purchased fillets of a different size, plan on 10 minutes per 1 inch (2.5 cm) of thickness.

5. Remove the baking sheet from the oven and slide the packets onto individual plates. Using kitchen scissors and keeping your fingers safely clear of the steam, cut around the edge of each packet and lift off the top paper or foil. Serve at once.

SERVES 4

NUTRITIONAL ANALYSIS PER SERVING
Calories 227 (Kilojoules 953); Protein 30 g; Carbohydrates 8 g; Total Fat 8 g; Saturated Fat 4 g; Cholesterol 97 mg; Sodium 377 mg; Dietary Fiber 2 g

Porter-Glazed Cornish Hens

½ cup (4 fl oz/125 ml) porter

2 tablespoons hoisin sauce

2 tablespoons honey

1 tablespoon tamari

4 Cornish hens, each about 1¼ lb (625 g)

½ teaspoon coarse salt

½ teaspoon freshly ground pepper

2 green (spring) onions, finely julienned

Many of the Pacific Northwest's fine microbreweries produce porter, a dark brown ale with a rounded flavor. When this robust beverage is blended with Chinese hoisin sauce, the result is a glaze that gives these hens a dark, rich flavor and glossy sheen. Serve the hens with Gai Lan with Crispy Garlic (page 92) and plenty of steamed rice.

1. Preheat the oven to 375°F (190°C).

2. In a large bowl or lock-top plastic bag, mix together the porter, hoisin, honey, and tamari. Add the hens and turn to coat. Marinate the hens at room temperature for 20 minutes, turning them occasionally.

3. Lift the hens from the marinade, reserving the marinade, and place them, breast side up, on a rack in a roasting pan. Spoon some of the marinade into the cavities and truss the hens closed. Sprinkle evenly with the salt and pepper.

4. Roast, basting several times with the remaining marinade, until the juices run clear when a thigh is pierced or until an instant-read thermometer inserted into the thickest part of the thigh reads 170°–175°F (77°–80°C), about 1 hour. Stop basting at least 15 minutes before the hens are done, discarding any remaining marinade. Transfer the hens to a platter, cover loosely, and let rest for 5 minutes.

5. Sprinkle the hens with the green onions and serve.

SERVES 4

NUTRITIONAL ANALYSIS PER SERVING
Calories 685 (Kilojoules 2,877); Protein 54 g; Carbohydrates 15 g; Total Fat 43 g; Saturated Fat 12 g; Cholesterol 312 mg; Sodium 748 mg; Dietary Fiber 0 g

In 1979, when a federal law declared the brewing of beer at home legal, Northwest home brewers emerged from their garages and basements, and the microbrew movement was born. Within a couple of years, the Red Hook Brewery of Washington and the Bridgeport, Widmer, Portland, and Full Sail brewing companies of Oregon had all opened their doors. Originally tiny microbreweries, today they are among the largest craft breweries in the country.

Craft beers and microbrews may come from large or small breweries and are terms now used interchangeably. Typically made with malted barley, hops, yeast, and water, craft beers, which range from lightly hopped lagers to dark, rich porters, avoid the additives such as corn or rice commonly used by large industrial operations.

A fine example of one of Oregon's smaller breweries is Hair of the Dog, which operates out of a gritty warehouse in Portland. The brewery's first two ales, Adambier and Golden Rose, are big, heavy beers with a walloping 8 to 10 percent alcohol content. Now producing about one thousand barrels a year,

Craft **Beers**

Hair of the Dog has a faithful and enthusiastic following.

Today, Oregon, with more than one thousand beers brewed in the state, boasts the largest number of breweries and brew pubs per capita in the United States. With menus developed to complement their handmade products, brew pubs serve up pizza and burgers, as well as salmon and pasta.

3 Vegetables, Grains & Beans

The Northwest is a paradise for all manner of vegetables. Because of its northern latitude, it is blessed with long summer days and, usually, summer sun. West of the Cascades, generous rains and a mild winter keep vegetable gardens producing all year long, perfect for sturdy greens, cabbages, and garlic. East of the Cascades, where summer temperatures are hot, bell peppers (capsicums), corn, and tomatoes thrive. With the simplest of preparations, these uncommonly good Northwest vegetables combine perfectly with local seafood and meats, as well as the many grains, pasta, and beans that have seduced the palates of the Pacific Northwest. As always, cook according to the season. Save the Squash and Barley Risotto (page 108) for the coldest months, and opt for the Penne with Morels and Spring Vegetables (page 84) in the spring. And if you are a crabber, make the Spaghetti with Dungeness Crab Sauce (page 96) anytime you get lucky.

Penne with Morels and Spring Vegetables

¼ cup (2 fl oz/60 ml) extra-virgin olive oil

2 oz (60 g) fresh morel or other flavorful wild or cultivated mushrooms (about 6 large), rinsed quickly or wiped clean, and halved if large

1 leek, including tender pale greens, finely julienned

2 oz (60 g) prosciutto, diced

¼ teaspoon red pepper flakes

1 bunch Swiss chard, about ¾ lb (375 g), leaves finely shredded and stems cut into 1-inch (2.5-cm) pieces

table salt to taste

1 lb (500 g) asparagus, tough ends removed and cut into 1½-inch (4-cm) lengths

1 cup (5 oz/155 g) fresh or frozen baby lima beans

½ teaspoon coarse salt

1 lb (500 g) penne

grated zest of 1 lemon (2 teaspoons)

½ cup (2 oz/60 g) grated or shaved pecorino romano cheese

Morels, with their earthy mushroom flavor, make this spring pasta special. They grow all over the Northwest in the spring, but as with any wild mushroom, you should refrain from picking them unless you are, or are with, an expert forager.

1. In a large frying pan over medium-high heat, warm the olive oil. Add the mushrooms, leek, prosciutto, and red pepper flakes and cook, stirring occasionally, until the leek is soft, about 2 minutes. Stir in the chard leaves, cover, and cook, stirring occasionally, until the chard wilts, 3–4 minutes.

2. Meanwhile, bring a large saucepan three-fourths full of water to a rolling boil. Add table salt to taste and the chard stems and boil until tender, about 3 minutes. Scoop the stems out with a wire skimmer and add to the frying pan.

3. Add the asparagus to the boiling water and cook until tender, 2–3 minutes. The timing will depend upon the thickness of the spears. Scoop out the asparagus and add to the frying pan. Add the lima beans to the boiling water and cook until tender, about 4 minutes. Scoop out and add to the frying pan. Season the vegetables with the coarse salt and set aside; keep warm.

4. Add the penne to the boiling water and cook until al dente, about 10 minutes. Drain, reserving ½ cup (4 fl oz/125 ml) of the pasta water. Place the pasta and the reserved water in a large warmed serving bowl.

5. Pour the contents of the frying pan over the pasta, add the lemon zest and cheese, and toss well. Serve immediately.

SERVES 6

NUTRITIONAL ANALYSIS PER SERVING
Calories 490 (Kilojoules 2,058); Protein 21 g; Carbohydrates 70 g; Total Fat 15 g; Saturated Fat 4 g; Cholesterol 17 mg; Sodium 554 mg; Dietary Fiber 5 g

Walla Walla Onion Rings

vegetable oil for deep-frying

1 large Walla Walla or other sweet
    onion, sliced ¼ inch (6 mm) thick

⅔ cup (5 fl oz/160 ml) water

⅔ cup (3½ oz/105 g) all-purpose
    (plain) flour

1½ cups (3½ oz/105 g) panko

grated zest of 1 lime

1 teaspoon coarse salt

2 tablespoons chopped fresh cilantro
    (fresh coriander)

lime wedges

The Japanese bread crumbs known as panko make the coating for these onion rings astonishingly light and crunchy. For entertaining, coat and fry the rings ahead of time and reheat them just before serving in a 350°F (180°C) oven for 10 minutes. The crunch will return.

1. Pour vegetable oil into a deep, heavy saucepan to a depth of 2 inches (5 cm) and heat to 375°F (190°C) on a deep-frying thermometer. Preheat the oven to 250°F (120°C). Line a baking sheet with paper towels.

2. Separate the onion slices into rings. In a bowl, whisk together the water and flour until smooth. Spread the panko on a plate.

3. When the oil reaches the correct temperature, dip the onion rings, 4 or 5 at a time, into the batter. Lift out, let the excess batter drip off, and then dip the rings in the crumbs, coating evenly. Slip the rings into the oil and fry, flipping them once to brown evenly, until golden brown, 1–2 minutes. Transfer to the lined baking sheet and place in the oven. Repeat until all the rings are cooked.

4. Transfer the rings to a platter and sprinkle with the lime zest, salt, and cilantro. Serve immediately with lime wedges.

SERVES 4

NUTRITIONAL ANALYSIS PER SERVING
Calories 343 (Kilojoules 1,441); Protein 8 g; Carbohydrates 45 g; Total Fat 15 g;
Saturated Fat 2 g; Cholesterol 0 mg; Sodium 454 mg; Dietary Fiber 3 g

Lentils with Browned Onions

2 large Walla Walla or other sweet onions

1½ cups (10½ oz/330 g) brown or green lentils

4 fresh thyme sprigs

⅓ cup (3 fl oz/80 ml) extra-virgin olive oil

¾ teaspoon coarse salt

¾ teaspoon freshly ground pepper

The Palouse region of eastern Washington and northern Idaho is famous for its dried peas and lentils. Every September, residents of Pullman, Washington, celebrate the lentil harvest with the National Lentil Festival. Here's one delicious and simple way to enjoy the versatile legume.

1. Cut the onions in half lengthwise. Cut the halves crosswise into slices ¼ inch (6 mm) thick.

2. Pick over the lentils, discarding any misshapen ones or stones, rinse well, and place in a large saucepan. Add water to cover by 2 inches (5 cm) and add the thyme sprigs. Bring to a boil over high heat, reduce the heat to medium-low, and simmer gently until very tender, about 25 minutes.

3. Meanwhile, cook the onions: In a large frying pan over medium-high heat, warm the olive oil. Add the onions and cook, stirring frequently, until dark brown, about 15 minutes. Stir in ¼ teaspoon each of the salt and pepper. Remove from the heat, cover, and keep warm.

4. Remove the lentils from the heat and remove and discard the thyme sprigs. Drain the lentils well, return them to the saucepan, and stir in the remaining ½ teaspoon each salt and pepper and half of the onions. Transfer the lentil mixture to a serving platter. Top with the remaining onions and serve immediately.

SERVES 4

NUTRITIONAL ANALYSIS PER SERVING
Calories 458 (Kilojoules 1,924); Protein 23 g; Carbohydrates 53 g; Total Fat 19 g; Saturated Fat 3 g; Cholesterol 0 mg; Sodium 296 mg; Dietary Fiber 11 g

Smashed Potatoes with Garlic

1 head garlic

1 tablespoon water

1½ lb (750 g) heirloom, Yellow Finn, or thin-skinned russet potatoes, unpeeled, cut into 1-inch (2.5-cm) chunks

1½ teaspoons coarse salt

¼ cup (2 fl oz/60 ml) extra-virgin olive oil

½ teaspoon freshly ground pepper

8 fresh basil leaves, finely shredded

In the summer and fall, I make this dish with some of the wonderful heirloom potatoes I buy at Seattle's University District farmers' market. Each variety has its own special color, texture, and flavor, but they all blend superbly with the heady bouquet of roasted garlic. Make sure to use your best extra-virgin olive oil here.

1. Preheat the oven to 450°F (230°C).

2. Remove the outer papery sheaths from the garlic head and cut off about 1 inch (2.5 cm) from the top to expose the cloves. Place the head on a double thickness of aluminum foil, sprinkle with the water, and wrap tightly. Roast until the cloves are very soft when squeezed, 30–40 minutes. Remove from the oven and reserve.

3. While the garlic is cooking, place the potatoes in a saucepan and add water to cover by 1 inch (2.5 cm) and 1 teaspoon of the coarse salt. Bring to a boil over high heat, reduce the heat to medium, and simmer, uncovered, until very tender, about 10 minutes. Drain the potatoes well, return them to the same pan, and place over low heat. Shake the pan back and forth over the heat to help dry the potatoes, about 2 minutes.

4. Squeeze all the garlic purée into the potatoes, then add the olive oil, the remaining ½ teaspoon coarse salt, and the pepper. Using a potato masher, mash lightly (the potatoes should retain plenty of lumps), mixing in the other ingredients at the same time.

5. Transfer the potatoes to a warmed bowl and top with the basil. Serve immediately.

SERVES 4

NUTRITIONAL ANALYSIS PER SERVING
Calories 275 (Kilojoules 1,155); Protein 4 g; Carbohydrates 34 g; Total Fat 14 g; Saturated Fat 2 g; Cholesterol 0 mg; Sodium 567 mg; Dietary Fiber 3 g

Manila Clam and Zucchini Risotto

Clams and zucchini make a wonderful risotto. Look for the sweet Manila clams so abundant in the Northwest.

1. Place the clams in a large saucepan, discarding any that fail to close to the touch. Add the wine, cover, and bring to a boil over high heat. Cook, shaking the pan occasionally, until the clams open, 5–10 minutes. Lift the lid from time to time and, using a slotted spoon, lift out the clams as they open, dropping them into a bowl. Discard any that failed to open. Pour the liquid through a fine-mesh sieve lined with cheesecloth (muslin); you should have about ½ cup (4 fl oz/125 ml). Remove the clams from the shells and chop coarsely; reserve. Wipe out the pan.

2. Combine the reserved clam liquid and the bottled juice or broth. Add enough water to make 5 cups (40 fl oz/1.25 l) total and pour into a small saucepan. Place over medium-low heat and bring to a bare simmer.

3. In the large saucepan over medium-high heat, melt the butter. Add the onion and garlic and cook, stirring often, until the onion is golden, 6–7 minutes. Stir in the zucchini and ½ cup (4 fl oz/125 ml) of the hot liquid and cover. Reduce the heat to medium and simmer until the zucchini are beginning to soften, about 8 minutes.

4. Uncover and stir in the rice. Cook, stirring, until the grains are well coated with butter. Add a ladleful of the hot liquid and simmer, stirring continuously, until absorbed. Add another ladleful of liquid, stirring continuously. Continue in this manner, adding a ladleful of liquid at a time and cooking until almost absorbed, until the rice is firm but tender and the center of each kernel is no longer chalky, about 20 minutes. (If you run out of liquid before the rice is ready, add hot water.)

5. Stir in the clams, parsley, salt, and pepper and transfer to a serving dish. Serve immediately.

SERVES 4

NUTRITIONAL ANALYSIS PER SERVING
Calories 440 (Kilojoules 1,848); Protein 20 g; Carbohydrates 68 g; Total Fat 8 g; Saturated Fat 4 g; Cholesterol 46 mg; Sodium 822 mg; Dietary Fiber 7 g

24 Manila or littleneck clams, scrubbed

½ cup (4 fl oz/125 ml) dry white wine

3½ cups (28 fl oz/875 ml) bottled clam juice or chicken stock

2 tablespoons unsalted butter

1 large Walla Walla or other sweet onion, chopped

2 cloves garlic, minced

1½ lb (750 g) zucchini (courgettes), trimmed and sliced ½ inch (12 mm) thick

1½ cups (10½ oz/330 g) Arborio rice

2 tablespoons chopped fresh flat-leaf (Italian) parsley

½ teaspoon salt

½ teaspoon freshly ground pepper

Gai Lan with Crispy Garlic

2 tablespoons canola oil

3 cloves garlic, thinly sliced

¼ teaspoon red pepper flakes

1 large bunch gai lan, 1½ lb (750 g),
tough stem ends trimmed

3 tablespoons rice wine or dry white
wine

2 tablespoons tamari

Most Northwest farmers' markets offer lots of different Asian vegetables, many of which are excellent for stir-frying. Gai lan (Chinese broccoli) is delicious cooked this way, but you can substitute bok choy, broccoli, or broccoli rabe as well. Make sure to cook the garlic just until golden; if it burns, you may not enjoy its taste.

1. Place a large frying pan or wok over high heat. When the pan is hot, add the canola oil and swirl the pan to coat the bottom. When the oil is very hot but not smoking, add the garlic and red pepper flakes and cook, stirring constantly, until the garlic is golden, about 1 minute. Using a slotted spoon, transfer the garlic to paper towels to drain.

2. Add the gai lan and 2 tablespoons of the wine and cook, tossing and stirring to prevent scorching, until tender, about 5 minutes. Add the tamari and the remaining 1 tablespoon wine and stir until the liquid reduces slightly, about 1 minute longer.

3. Transfer the gai lan to a warmed platter, sprinkle with the reserved garlic, and serve immediately.

SERVES 4

NUTRITIONAL ANALYSIS PER SERVING
Calories 112 (Kilojoules 470); Protein 5 g; Carbohydrates 8 g; Total Fat 7 g;
Saturated Fat 1 g; Cholesterol 0 mg; Sodium 582 mg; Dietary Fiber 3 g

Macaroni and Cheese with Onions

4 thick slices bacon, about ¼ lb (125 g) total weight

3 tablespoons unsalted butter

1 small Walla Walla or other sweet onion, finely chopped

1½ cups (3 oz/90 g) fresh bread crumbs

1½ teaspoons chopped fresh thyme

¾ teaspoon coarse salt, plus salt to taste

¾ teaspoon freshly ground pepper

1 lb (500 g) large elbow macaroni

2 tablespoons all-purpose (plain) flour

2 cups (16 fl oz/500 ml) low-fat or skim milk

4 cups (1 lb/500 g) shredded sharp cheddar cheese

This rich dish is pure comfort food, perfect for a cold, wet June day when the season's first Walla Walla onions appear in the market. I use Oregon's Bandon organic cheddar, but any of the fine Tillamook or Cougar Gold cheddars would work, too.

1. Preheat the oven to 350°F (180°C). Grease a 1½-qt (1.5-l) baking dish with butter.

2. In a frying pan over medium-high heat, fry the bacon until crisp, 6–8 minutes. Using a fork, transfer to paper towels to drain, then chop coarsely. Discard all but 1 tablespoon of the drippings from the pan.

3. Return the pan to medium-high heat and add 1 tablespoon of the butter. When it melts, stir in the onion and cook, stirring often, until golden, 3–4 minutes. Stir in the bread crumbs, bacon, thyme, and ¼ teaspoon each of the salt and pepper. Remove from the heat.

4. Meanwhile, bring a large saucepan three-fourths full of water to a boil. Add salt to taste and the macaroni, stir well, and cook until al dente, 8–10 minutes. Drain well and pour into the prepared baking dish.

5. In a small saucepan over medium heat, melt the remaining 2 tablespoons butter. When it melts, whisk in the flour and continue to whisk for 1 minute. Gradually whisk in the milk until smooth. Simmer, stirring occasionally, until lightly thickened, 2–3 minutes. Whisk in the cheese until melted and smooth. Add the remaining ½ teaspoon each salt and pepper and pour over the macaroni. Sprinkle evenly with the bread-crumb mixture.

6. Bake the macaroni until the topping is lightly browned and the mixture is bubbling, 35–40 minutes. Serve hot directly from the dish.

SERVES 6

NUTRITIONAL ANALYSIS PER SERVING
Calories 779 (Kilojoules 3,272); Protein 35 g; Carbohydrates 72 g; Total Fat 38 g; Saturated Fat 22 g; Cholesterol 107 mg; Sodium 867 mg; Dietary Fiber 3 g

From June through August, the sweet, creamy globes known as Walla Walla onions grace the marketplace. Similar to the Vidalia, Maui, and Texas 1015 Supersweet, Walla Walla onions are high in moisture and low in sulfur (only about half the amount of most onions). This combination gives the onion its illusion of pure sweetness.

Although Walla Wallas have been grown in the United States for nearly a century, the seed originated on the French island of Corsica. Introduced by a Frenchman, Peter Pieri, to the southeast Washington town of Walla Walla, it was quickly embraced by the local Italian-American farmers. John Arbini hand-selected his stock and developed an onion of remarkable sweetness, the Yellow Globe. Although the name didn't stick, his stock did and later became known as the Walla Walla Sweet.

In May 1995, a federally protected growing area, similar to the French *appellation d'origin contrôlée* system for wines, was designated to protect Walla Walla onions. Thus, Walla Wallas can be marketed as such only if grown in the Walla Walla Valley of southeast Washington and northeast Oregon.

Walla Walla **Onions**

When these delicate seasonal beauties appear, use them quickly, as their shelf life is short. They are wonderful raw, deep-fried, or roasted, or used in relishes and chutneys. Although some enthusiasts insist that the onion can be eaten like an apple, others find this a bit extreme. As sweet as Walla Wallas are, they are still, after all, onions.

Spaghetti with Dungeness Crab Sauce

1 whole Dungeness crab, cooked
and cooled

2 tablespoons extra-virgin olive oil

2 cloves garlic, thinly sliced

pinch of red pepper flakes

1 can (28 oz/875 g) whole tomatoes
with juice

1 can (14 oz/440 g) chopped plum
(Roma) tomatoes with juice

½ teaspoon coarse salt

1 lb (500 g) spaghetti

2 tablespoons chopped fresh basil

In the Northwest, cooked Dungeness crabs are available year-round, in every fish store and supermarket, making this an easy dish to prepare. If you like, ask the fishmonger to clean the crab for you. Just be sure to save the shell along with the crabmeat, as you'll need both for the sauce.

1. Remove the crab carapace, the bony shield covering the back, and rinse. Crack and clean the crab, removing the meat to a bowl and reserving the shells. Refrigerate the meat.

2. Break up the carapace and collect all the shell pieces in a 12-inch (30-cm) square of cheesecloth (muslin). Tie the ends together with kitchen string and set aside.

3. In a large saucepan over medium-high heat, warm the olive oil. Add the garlic and red pepper flakes and sauté until the garlic is golden, about 1 minute. Add the cheesecloth packet of crab shells, the whole and chopped tomatoes with their juice, breaking up the tomatoes with a wooden spoon, and the salt. Bring to a boil, reduce the heat to medium, and simmer, uncovered, until lightly thickened, about 40 minutes. Lift out the packet of crab shells (let any juices drain back into the pan) and discard.

4. Meanwhile, bring another large saucepan three-fourths full of salted water to a rolling boil. Add the spaghetti, stir well, and boil until half cooked, 4–6 minutes. Drain well and return the spaghetti to the same pan.

5. Pour the tomato sauce over the spaghetti and continue cooking over medium-high heat, stirring frequently, until the spaghetti is al dente, 3–5 minutes longer. Add the crabmeat, stir well, and remove from the heat.

6. Divide the pasta among warmed individual dishes and sprinkle with the basil. Serve immediately.

SERVES 4

NUTRITIONAL ANALYSIS PER SERVING
Calories 579 (Kilojoules 2,432); Protein 25 g; Carbohydrates 98 g; Total Fat 9 g;
Saturated Fat 1 g; Cholesterol 24 mg; Sodium 797 mg; Dietary Fiber 5 g

Wine
Making

The beginnings of the Northwest wine industry can be traced to Fort Vancouver, on the shore of the Columbia River in Washington State. There, in 1825, Dr. John McLoughlin, the leader of the local Hudson's Bay outpost, planted Black Hamburg and Black Prince grapes. Both flourished.

The fort's young vines were the first of many. By 1836, French-Canadian settlers living near Walla Walla, Washington, were not only growing grapes, but producing wine as well. Soon, cuttings from California and Europe were helping to accelerate the burgeoning industry.

Unfortunately, with the enactment of Prohibition in 1919, commercial wine production was effectively ended. Many grapevines were plowed under and replanted with fruit trees. But with the repeal of Prohibition in 1933, Washington quickly licensed its first winery. Within five years, Washington counted forty-two licensed wineries and Oregon twenty-eight.

The Northwest's great wine expansion began in the 1970s and included the predecessors of today's Chateau Ste. Michelle and Columbia Winery, both of Woodinville, Washington, as well as Hillcrest Winery of Roseburg,

Oregon. With regular press reports touting the Northwest's fledgling vineyards, winery development in both states was soon under way. In Oregon, David Lett of The Eyrie Vineyards, Dick Erath of Erath Vineyards, and Scott Henry of Henry Estate Winery were leaders. In Washington, Preston Wine Cellars and Hogue Cellars opened in the southeast corner of the state.

Today, the majority of Oregon's vineyards lie west of the Cascades in the Willamette, Umpqua, and Rogue Valleys. These areas have temperate marine microclimates, which means the grapes experience a long, gentle ripening. The majority of Washington's vineyards are located east of the Cascades in the Columbia and Yakima Valleys, where long, hot days and cool nights bring the fruit to the peak of ripeness.

Oregon has many showcase wines, but its signature is Pinot Noir. While young, Oregon Pinot is a lusciously fruity red wine; when aged, it develops wonderful complexity. As far as Oregon whites are concerned, the best include Pinot Gris, Chardonnay, White Riesling, Gewürztraminer, Sauvignon Blanc, and Müller-Thurgau, a wine with a low-acid, mild flavor.

Washington State is second only to California in wine grape production within the United States. At one time known mainly for its Rieslings, Washington is now recognized for its Chardonnays. Crisp and delicate, the wines often have a light oak cast. Well-known Washington reds include Merlot, with sweet cherry and berry flavors; Cabernet Sauvignon; Cabernet Franc; Syrah; and Lemberger.

Some fine examples of Northwest wines (opposite). Known for Pinot Noir, Cristom and Erath Vineyards of Oregon's Willamette Valley also produce some fine whites, including Pinot Gris and Chardonnay. Chehalem Vineyard in Newberg, Oregon (below), boasts a delicious Pinot Noir.

Beets and Beans with Hazelnuts

3 large red or golden beets, about 1½ lb (750 g) total weight

1 tablespoon water

2 tablespoons hazelnuts (filberts)

¼ lb (125 g) sugar snap peas, trimmed

¼ lb (125 g) green beans, trimmed and cut into 2-inch (5-cm) lengths

2 teaspoons olive oil

½ teaspoon coarse salt

½ teaspoon freshly ground pepper

1 tablespoon hazelnut oil or walnut oil

2 teaspoons sherry vinegar

Hazelnuts blend beautifully with the sweet, earthy taste of beets. Toss in green beans, sugar snaps, and a tangy sherry vinaigrette, and you have a wonderful warm salad. If available, use a combination of red, Chioggia, and golden beets.

1. Preheat the oven to 400°F (200°C).

2. Trim off the greens from each beet, leaving ½ inch (12 mm) of the stem intact. Reserve the greens for another use. Scrub the beets but do not peel. Place in a baking dish and add the water. Cover tightly with aluminum foil and bake until very tender, 45–60 minutes. Remove from the oven and let cool a bit.

3. While the beets are baking, spread the hazelnuts on a baking sheet and toast in the same oven until the skins have blackened and the nuts are lightly browned, about 15 minutes. Transfer the still-warm nuts to a kitchen towel and rub briskly to remove the skins (don't worry if a few flecks remain). Chop coarsely and set aside.

4. Raise the oven temperature to 450°F (230°C).

5. In a bowl, combine the sugar snap peas and the green beans. Add the olive oil and ¼ teaspoon each of the salt and pepper. Toss to coat the beans and peas well and then turn out onto a baking sheet, spreading them in a single layer. Roast until tender, about 10 minutes.

6. While the beans are roasting, slip the skins off the beets. Quarter the beets through their stem ends, then slice the quarters crosswise into slices ¼ inch (6 mm) thick. Place in a bowl. When the snap peas and green beans are ready, add them to the bowl.

7. In a small bowl, whisk together the hazelnut or walnut oil, vinegar, and the remaining ¼ teaspoon each salt and pepper. Pour over the vegetables and sprinkle with the hazelnuts. Toss well and serve at once.

SERVES 4

NUTRITIONAL ANALYSIS PER SERVING
Calories 123 (Kilojoules 517); Protein 3 g; Carbohydrates 11 g; Total Fat 8 g; Saturated Fat 1 g; Cholesterol 0 mg; Sodium 234 mg; Dietary Fiber 2 g

Russet and Sweet Potatoes

1½ lb (750 g) russet potatoes, peeled and cut into 1-inch (2.5-cm) pieces

1 lb (500 g) sweet potatoes, peeled and cut into 1½-inch (4-cm) pieces

salt to taste, plus 1 teaspoon

¼ cup (2 fl oz/60 ml) buttermilk

3 tablespoons unsalted butter

1 tablespoon blackberry honey

½ teaspoon freshly ground pepper

2 tablespoons thinly sliced fresh chives or green (spring) onion tops

My local food cooperative always stocks organic Jewel or Red Garnet sweet potatoes (sometimes mislabeled as yams), which are perfect for this dish. Each has a lovely color and flavor and blends beautifully with Idaho's famed russet potatoes and the tang of buttermilk. If you can't locate blackberry honey, use another mild-flavored honey.

1. Place the russet potatoes and sweet potatoes in a large saucepan and add water to cover by 1 inch (2.5 cm) and salt to taste. Bring to a boil over high heat, reduce the heat to medium, and simmer, uncovered, until very tender, about 8 minutes. Drain the potatoes well and pass them through a food mill or potato ricer placed over the same saucepan. Place the pan over low heat and stir the potatoes to dry them slightly, about 2 minutes.

2. Stir in the buttermilk, butter, honey, the 1 teaspoon salt, and the pepper, mixing well. Transfer to a warmed serving dish and top with the chives or green onion tops. Serve immediately.

SERVES 4

NUTRITIONAL ANALYSIS PER SERVING
Calories 309 (Kilojoules 1,298); Protein 5 g; Carbohydrates 53 g; Total Fat 9 g; Saturated Fat 5 g; Cholesterol 24 mg; Sodium 623 mg; Dietary Fiber 5 g

Cranberry Beans with Oregano

2½ lb (1.25 kg) fresh cranberry
    (borlotti) beans, or 1¼ cups
    (9 oz/280 g) dried cranberry beans

2 bay leaves

4 garlic cloves

1¼ teaspoons coarse salt

3 tablespoons extra-virgin olive oil

½ teaspoon freshly ground pepper

1 tablespoon chopped fresh oregano

Cranberry beans, marbled with purple and white when raw, become an antique mauve when cooked. They have a warm and nutty flavor. Here, they are paired with garlic, oregano, and extra-virgin olive oil to make a simple side dish to accompany grilled salmon or steak. For a main dish, try tossing the beans with cooked pasta, chopped tomatoes, and a sprinkling of Parmesan.

1. If using fresh cranberry beans, pop them from the shells. Place them in a large saucepan with water to cover by 2 inches (5 cm); add the bay leaves and garlic. If using dried cranberry beans, pick them over, discarding any misshapen beans or stones. Rinse well, place in a bowl, add water to cover generously, and let soak overnight. The next day, drain and place in a large saucepan with water to cover by 2 inches (5 cm); add the bay leaves and garlic. Bring the fresh or dried beans to a boil over high heat, reduce the heat to medium-low, and simmer gently, uncovered, until the beans are tender, about 30 minutes for fresh beans and 1 hour for dried beans.

2. Remove from the heat and add 1 teaspoon of the salt. Stir well and let stand for 10 minutes.

3. Drain the beans well and remove and discard the bay leaves. Stir in the olive oil, the remaining ¼ teaspoon salt, the pepper, and the oregano, mashing the garlic as you stir. Transfer to a platter and serve at once.

SERVES 4

NUTRITIONAL ANALYSIS PER SERVING
Calories 311 (Kilojoules 1,306); Protein 15 g; Carbohydrates 40 g; Total Fat 11 g;
Saturated Fat 2 g; Cholesterol 0 mg; Sodium 464 mg; Dietary Fiber 6 g

Kale with Browned Butter Crumbs

Nowadays, different varieties of kale regularly show up at market. Red Russian has flattish leaves with red and purple markings and reddish purplish ribs. Lacinato, sometimes called Dinosaur kale, is black-green with long, slender leaves. Curly kale is all green, with ruffly short leaves and tough green stems. All of these varieties flourish in the damp, cool weather of the Pacific Northwest.

¾ teaspoon coarse salt

1 large bunch kale, 1¼ lb (625 g), stems and ribs removed and leaves cut up

2 teaspoons fresh lemon juice

¼ cup (2 oz/60 g) unsalted butter

1 cup (2 oz/60 g) fresh bread crumbs

¼ teaspoon freshly ground pepper

1 teaspoon grated lemon zest

1. Pour water to a depth of ¼ inch (6 mm) into a large frying pan and place over high heat. Add ½ teaspoon of the salt and the kale, cover, and cook the leaves, turning them several times, until they are tender, about 10 minutes.

2. Drain the kale well, transfer to a serving platter, and toss with the lemon juice. Cover and keep warm.

3. Meanwhile, in a small frying pan over medium heat, melt the butter and cook, stirring occasionally, until medium brown, about 10 minutes. Stir in the bread crumbs and cook, stirring frequently, until crisp, 2–3 minutes. Stir in the remaining ¼ teaspoon salt, the pepper, and the lemon zest.

4. Sprinkle the bread crumbs over the kale and serve immediately.

SERVES 4

NUTRITIONAL ANALYSIS PER SERVING
Calories 185 (Kilojoules 777); Protein 4 g; Carbohydrates 16 g; Total Fat 13 g;
Saturated Fat 7 g; Cholesterol 32 mg; Sodium 385 mg; Dietary Fiber 2 g

Potato and Fennel Gratin

2 fennel bulbs

2 tablespoons extra-virgin olive oil

1 Walla Walla or other sweet onion, thinly sliced

¾ teaspoon coarse salt

¾ teaspoon freshly ground pepper

2 lb (1 kg) russet potatoes, peeled and sliced ⅛ inch (3 mm) thick

1 cup (4 oz/125 g) grated Parmesan cheese

½ cup (4 fl oz/125 ml) chicken stock

½ cup (4 fl oz/125 ml) heavy (double) cream

Made with sweetly flavored Florence (bulb) fennel and the Northwest's Walla Walla onions, this rich gratin makes a truly special dinner when served with a roasted chicken and salad. Perfect for entertaining: simply assemble the gratin 3 hours ahead, cover, and refrigerate until cooking time.

1. Trim off the feathery tops from the fennel bulbs and reserve. Remove the stalks and any tough or bruised outer leaves from the bulbs and discard. Cut in half lengthwise, then thinly slice lengthwise.

2. In a large frying pan over medium heat, warm the olive oil. Add the onion and sliced fennel and cook, stirring frequently, until the vegetables are very tender, about 20 minutes. Season with half each of the salt and pepper. Remove from the heat. Chop 2 tablespoons of the reserved fennel fronds, add to the frying pan, and stir well.

3. Preheat the oven to 375°F (190°C).

4. Place half of the fennel mixture on the bottom of a 2½-qt (2.5-l) gratin dish or baking dish. Top with half of the potatoes and sprinkle with half of the remaining salt and pepper. Top with the remaining fennel mixture and sprinkle with half of the Parmesan cheese. Top with the remaining potatoes and then sprinkle with the remaining salt and pepper. Pour the chicken stock and the cream evenly over the surface and sprinkle with the remaining Parmesan cheese.

5. Cover tightly with aluminum foil and bake for 30 minutes. Uncover and continue to bake until the potatoes are cooked through when tested with a knife and the top is nicely browned, about 45 minutes longer. Remove from the oven and let stand for 5 minutes.

6. To serve, scoop out with a large serving spoon at table.

SERVES 6

NUTRITIONAL ANALYSIS PER SERVING
Calories 336 (Kilojoules 1,411); Protein 13 g; Carbohydrates 32 g; Total Fat 18 g; Saturated Fat 9 g; Cholesterol 42 mg; Sodium 699 mg; Dietary Fiber 4 g

Born in Portland, Oregon, in 1903, James Andrew Beard has been affectionately hailed as the Father of American Gastronomy. Although he was a student of theater and voice, his attempts to make it as a performer were largely unsuccessful, a failure that will forever benefit American cuisine.

He received excellent informal culinary training—and a passion for good food—from his mother, Elizabeth, who ran a boardinghouse. Summers found the Beards on the Oregon coast, dining happily on Dungeness crabs, salmon, sturgeon, oysters, and wild berries.

Settling in New York City, Beard began a catering business, followed by a shop specializing in hors d'oeuvres. In time he became an influential member of the culinary community, publishing twenty-two cookbooks, many of them still classics.

In 1955, Beard established The James Beard Cooking School, with branches in New York and Seaside, Oregon. For the next thirty years, he brought his message of simple, good food, using the freshest local and seasonal ingredients, to cooking schools and civic groups alike. After his death in 1985, a

James **Beard**

foundation was established in his name, dedicated to the promotion of fine food and drink and culinary scholarship and to fostering the talents of chefs from across the country. Although Beard lived much of his life in New York, his writing returned again and again to the rich food memories of his Northwest childhood.

Squash and Barley Risotto

6 cups (48 fl oz/1.5 l) vegetable or
chicken stock

2 tablespoons unsalted butter

2 carrots, peeled and finely chopped

2 shallots, minced

½ lb (250 g) fresh cremini mushrooms, brushed clean and thinly
sliced

1 cup (8 oz/250 g) pearl barley

1 small butternut squash, about 1½ lb
(750 g), peeled, seeded, and cut
into 1-inch (2.5-cm) chunks

1 bay leaf

½ teaspoon coarse salt

½ teaspoon freshly ground pepper

½ cup (2 oz/60 g) walnut halves

½ cup (2 oz/60 g) grated Parmesan
cheese

2 tablespoons thinly sliced fresh
chives

This wintry dish makes a lovely meal accompanied with a crusty artisan bread, a green salad, and a Northwest Chardonnay. I call it *risotto* for the style in which it's made. Pearl barley makes an excellent substitute for the Arborio rice that's traditionally used. If you have wild mushrooms on hand, use them in place of the cremini.

1. Pour the stock into a saucepan and bring to a simmer. Adjust the heat so the liquid maintains a bare simmer.

2. In a large saucepan over medium-high heat, melt the butter. Add the carrots and shallots and cook, stirring frequently, until the shallots are soft, 2–3 minutes. Add the mushrooms and cook, stirring frequently, until tender, about 5 minutes. Stir in the barley and cook, stirring to coat the grains, for 1 minute longer. Add the squash and bay leaf and 2½ cups (20 fl oz/625 ml) of the hot stock. Cover and simmer until the stock is absorbed, about 10 minutes.

3. Uncover and continue simmering, stirring in ½ cup (4 fl oz/125 ml) of the stock at a time and waiting for each addition to be absorbed before adding more. After 35–40 minutes, the barley should be creamy and tender. Season with the salt and pepper.

4. Meanwhile, in a small frying pan over medium-high heat, toast the walnuts until lightly browned, 5–7 minutes. Transfer to a cutting board and chop coarsely.

5. To serve, ladle the risotto into warmed individual bowls. Sprinkle with the Parmesan, walnuts, and chives and serve immediately.

SERVES 4

NUTRITIONAL ANALYSIS PER SERVING
Calories 535 (Kilojoules 2,247); Protein 21 g; Carbohydrates 73 g; Total Fat 20 g;
Saturated Fat 7 g; Cholesterol 27 mg; Sodium 1,196 mg; Dietary Fiber 14 g

Asparagus with Chive Vinaigrette

1½ lb (750 g) asparagus, tough
   stems removed

¼ cup (⅓ oz/10 g) chopped fresh
   chives

1 shallot, minced

2 teaspoons champagne vinegar or
   white wine vinegar

3 tablespoons extra-virgin olive oil

¼ teaspoon coarse salt

¼ teaspoon freshly ground pepper

organic edible blossoms, separated
   into petals

During asparagus season, people in the Northwest consume the tasty spears in many different guises: grilled, roasted, simmered, and steamed. Here, the asparagus are cooked quickly in a little water, dressed with a simple vinaigrette, and decorated with edible blossoms. I prefer chive blossoms, but you could use organic violets or nasturtiums as well.

1. Fill a large frying pan with water to a depth of ½ inch (12 mm) and place over high heat. Bring to a boil, add the asparagus, and cook until tender, 3–6 minutes. The timing will depend upon the thickness of the spears.

2. Meanwhile, in a small bowl, whisk together the chives, shallot, vinegar, olive oil, salt, and pepper to form a vinaigrette.

3. When the asparagus are ready, carefully lift them out of the water with tongs, draining them well, and place on a serving platter. Drizzle with the vinaigrette and sprinkle with the chive petals. Serve hot or at room temperature.

SERVES 6

NUTRITIONAL ANALYSIS PER SERVING
Calories 82 (Kilojoules 344); Protein 3 g; Carbohydrates 4 g; Total Fat 7 g;
Saturated Fat 1 g; Cholesterol 0 mg; Sodium 62 mg; Dietary Fiber 1 g

Polenta with Mushrooms and Hazelnuts

¼ cup (1¼ oz/37 g) hazelnuts (filberts)

2 tablespoons extra-virgin olive oil

1 lb (500 g) fresh cremini mushrooms, brushed clean and quartered

1 lb (500 g) fresh wild mushrooms such as chanterelle or oyster, rinsed quickly or brushed clean, and cut into ½-inch (12-mm) pieces

1 can (28 oz/875 g) plum (Roma) tomatoes, seeded and chopped, with juice reserved

2 cloves garlic, minced

½ teaspoon each coarse salt and freshly ground pepper

1 cup (5 oz/155 g) crumbled fresh goat cheese

2 tablespoons chopped fresh flat-leaf (Italian) parsley

POLENTA

3 cups (24 fl oz/750 ml) low-fat milk

4 cups (32 fl oz/1 l) water

2 teaspoons coarse salt

2 cups (10 oz/315 g) imported instant polenta

Northwest hazelnuts find their way into many local dishes, whether sweet or savory. Here, their warm, luscious flavor blends beautifully with this woodsy wild mushroom ragout. The same ragout also is delicious served over pasta.

1. Preheat the oven to 350°F (180°C). Spread the hazelnuts on a baking sheet and toast until the skins have blackened and the nuts are lightly browned, about 15 minutes. Transfer the still-warm nuts to a kitchen towel and rub briskly to remove the skins (don't worry if some flecks remain). Chop coarsely and set aside.

2. In a large frying pan over high heat, warm the olive oil. Add all of the mushrooms and cook, stirring occasionally, until they have browned and are starting to soften, about 5 minutes. Add the tomatoes and ½ cup (4 fl oz/ 125 ml) of the reserved tomato juice, garlic, salt, and pepper and cook, stirring, until the mushrooms are very tender, about 10 minutes longer.

3. To make the polenta, combine the milk, water, and salt in a heavy saucepan and bring to a boil over medium-high heat. Add the polenta slowly while whisking constantly in one direction. Switch to a wooden spoon and continue stirring until the polenta is thickened, 1–2 minutes.

4. Divide the polenta among warmed individual plates and top with the mushrooms. Sprinkle with the goat cheese, hazelnuts, and parsley. Serve immediately.

SERVES 4

NUTRITIONAL ANALYSIS PER SERVING
Calories 647 (Kilojoules 2,718); Protein 27 g; Carbohydrates 82 g; Total Fat 26 g; Saturated Fat 10 g; Cholesterol 35 mg; Sodium 1,524 mg; Dietary Fiber 12 g

W hen is a hazelnut a filbert and a filbert a hazelnut? Both names refer to the same nut, although much confusion cloaks the two monikers. Originally used in the United Kingdom, the name hazelnut arrived in this country with its earliest settlers. The name filbert, however, seems to be of French origin, although no one knows for sure. In 1989, Oregonians formally declared their preference with the designation of the hazelnut as the Official State Nut.

In fact, Oregon's Willamette Valley grows 99 percent of the national crop. With the planting of the New World's first tree in 1858 in Scottsburg, Oregon, the Northwest hazelnut industry was born. Today, a dozen varieties grow in the Pacific Northwest, with the nuts sold whole or shelled, roasted or raw, in addition to being pressed into oil.

The hazelnut is a versatile nut, easily playing a role in just about any meal. Each fall, the Essential Bread Bakery in Seattle bakes a loaf studded with ripe local pears, dried figs, and a healthy helping of hazelnuts. At Zefiro Restaurant in Portland, roasted quail are dusted with a coating of finely ground

Oregon **Hazelnuts**

hazelnuts and served with greens and a sauce of port and blackberries. The Bay Cafe on Lopez Island, Washington, prepares halibut encrusted in chopped hazelnuts. And at Fran's Chocolates in Seattle, a hazelnut paste from Dundee, Oregon, is transformed into *gianduia,* an Italian confection combining the rich paste with Venezuelan chocolate.

4 Desserts

At the height of a Northwest summer, desserts are always a pleasure to make. Indeed, the biggest dilemma is deciding which fruit to use. The bounty is quite breathtaking, from the gorgeous array of stone fruits to the glistening boxes of berries. Decisions don't seem to get any easier in the autumn, when bushels of crisp apples and juicy pears arrive. Make it easy on yourself, and choose the best and brightest. Substitute blackberries for raspberries, or apples for pears. And if the fruit decision is just too difficult, a batch of Espresso–Triple Chocolate Brownies (page 134) or a selection of the Northwest's fine chocolates are happy solutions.

Cherries in Port

2 tablespoons superfine (caster) sugar

½ cup (4 fl oz/125 ml) port

3 lemon zest strips, each 1 inch (2.5 cm) wide and 2 inches (5 cm) long

1¼ lb (625 g) ripe sweet cherries with stems

Whidbeys Washington Port, a vintage-dated port made from Columbia Valley grapes, is perfect for this easily prepared dish. The cherries are lightly flavored and refreshing after macerating for only 1 hour, although the longer you leave them, the more deliciously soused they become. Serve some fine Northwest chocolates on the side.

1. In a large bowl, stir together the sugar, port, and lemon zest. Add the cherries and toss well.

2. Cover and refrigerate for at least 1 hour or for up to 3 days, stirring several times.

3. To serve, place the cherries in a serving bowl and let diners grab them with their fingers. Have small bowls ready for the pits and stems.

SERVES 4

NUTRITIONAL ANALYSIS PER SERVING
Calories 163 (Kilojoules 685); Protein 2 g; Carbohydrates 31 g; Total Fat 1 g; Saturated Fat 0 g; Cholesterol 0 mg; Sodium 3 mg; Dietary Fiber 2 g

Coeur à la Crème with Blackberry Honey

½ lb (250 g) cream cheese (made without preservatives), at room temperature

2 oz (60 g) fresh goat cheese

3 tablespoons confectioners' (icing) sugar

½ cup (4 fl oz/125 ml) heavy (double) cream, softly whipped

30 dried apricot halves, snipped into small pieces

15 large pitted prunes, snipped into small pieces

¾ cup (6 fl oz/180 ml) medium-dry Gewürztraminer

3 tablespoons blackberry honey

Coeur à la crème, French for "heart of cream," is a classic dessert of sweetened fresh cheese prepared in a heart-shaped mold. For this recipe, you'll need a 6-inch (15-cm) coeur à la crème mold (measured point to point), which can be found at most kitchen stores or by mail order. Here I've combined cream cheese, heavy cream, and fresh goat cheese with excellent results.

1. In a food processor, combine the cream cheese, goat cheese, and confectioners' sugar. Process until blended. Scrape into a bowl.

2. In another bowl, using a whisk, whip the cream until soft peaks form. Fold the cream into the cheese mixture.

3. Dampen a 14-inch (35-cm) square of cheesecloth (muslin) and use it to line a coeur à la crème mold (see note). Fill the mold with the cheese mixture and fold the cheesecloth over the top. Set the mold on a plate and place in the refrigerator. Refrigerate for at least 4 hours or for up to overnight.

4. In a small nonaluminum saucepan over high heat, combine the apricots, prunes, Gewürztraminer, and honey and bring to a boil. Stir well, remove from the heat, cover, and let stand off the heat for 10 minutes. Then cover and refrigerate until serving time.

5. To serve, uncover the top of the mold and carefully invert the mold onto a serving plate. Lift off the mold and peel off the cheesecloth. Spoon a serving of cheese into individual bowls or plates and top with some of the fruit.

SERVES 6

NUTRITIONAL ANALYSIS PER SERVING
Calories 397 (Kilojoules 1,667); Protein 6 g; Carbohydrates 42 g; Total Fat 23 g; Saturated Fat 14 g; Cholesterol 73 mg; Sodium 159 mg; Dietary Fiber 3 g

One summer day, while bicycling on Lopez Island, Washington, I spied a small sign reading, "Homemade Pie, One Mile." I followed that sign and found farmhouse pies that were everything anyone could want: delicate crusts filled with warm, tart blackberries and topped with homemade ice cream. Although memory now fails me on the remainder of the day, I still remember those pies.

With its generous rainfall, temperate winters, and long summer days, the Northwest seems tailor-made for growing the countless varieties of berries that flourish here.

Strawberry plants are the first to bear fruit, beginning to ripen in late May. They belong to the genus *Fragaria,* the source of the word *fragrance,* and these Northwest berries are indeed wonderfully perfumed. They are best when eaten with just-baked shortbread and whipped cream.

Brambleberries, a category that includes raspberries and blackberries, are an important Northwest crop. Predominantly harvested in June, raspberries are sold fresh and also are processed as individually quick-frozen berries, raspberry purée, or

Baskets of
Berries

juice. The extraordinarily sweet raspberries that take over my vegetable garden occasionally make it onto oatmeal, but the majority are eaten on the spot. Black raspberries, also known as "blackcaps," are small, sweet natives.

Blackberries are divided into two main categories: the native trailing ground-cover plant, which produces small, intensely flavored berries, and a pair of naturalized Europeans, the Himalayan Giant and the Evergreen, both of which grow wild and vigorously throughout the Northwest. Two cultivated varieties, the marionberry and the thornless Evergreen, are always available in markets.

Hybrid crosses between blackberries and raspberries are an increasingly important segment of the cultivated crop. Some of the most popular are the boysenberry, loganberry, and tayberry. Moderately tart and large, these berries are wonderful in ice creams, sorbets, and pies.

The Northwest commercial blueberry business began in the late 1930s with transplants from New Jersey. These high bush berries thrive in our marine climate and are perfect in muffins, pies, and scones.

Other important berry crops are cranberries, gooseberries, and currants. Oregon began its cranberry cultivation in 1885, with vines from Massachusetts. Today, the crop is centered in the coastal town of Bandon, Oregon. Most of the nation's red currants and gooseberries are grown in the Northwest, although both crops are small relative to those of the region's other berries.

Blueberries, blackberries, raspberries, and gooseberries are but a few of the many types of berries grown in the Pacific Northwest.

Berry Fritters

1 cup (5 oz/155 g) all-purpose (plain) flour

2 tablespoons sugar, plus more for coating

1½ teaspoons baking powder

2 eggs, separated

⅔ cup (5 fl oz/160 ml) milk

finely grated zest of 1 lime

pinch of salt

1½ cups (6 oz/185 g) mixed berries such as blueberries, raspberries, and blackberries

canola oil for deep-frying

You can use a combination of berries for these fritters. It's important to keep the oil at 350°F (180°C) while frying; any lower and the fritters may end up with soggy centers. Slip a deep-frying thermometer into the oil to monitor its temperature from first batch to last.

1. Preheat the oven to 250°F (120°C).

2. In a large bowl, whisk together the flour, the 2 tablespoons sugar, and the baking powder. In a small bowl, lightly beat the egg yolks. Whisk them into the flour mixture along with the milk and lime zest, beating until smooth.

3. In another bowl, using an electric mixer, beat together the egg whites and salt until stiff peaks form. Using a rubber spatula, fold the egg whites into the batter just until no white streaks remain. Stir in the berries.

4. Spread additional sugar in a pie dish for coating the fritters after they are cooked. Pour canola oil into a deep frying pan to a depth of 2 inches (5 cm) and heat to 350°F (180°C) on a deep-frying thermometer. Working in batches, drop in the batter, 1 heaping tablespoon at a time. Cook until golden brown on the bottom, 2–3 minutes. Using a slotted spoon, turn the fritters and cook the other side until browned, about 2 minutes longer. With the slotted spoon, transfer to paper towels to drain briefly, then toss the fritters in the sugar until covered evenly. Transfer to a platter and place in the warm oven. Repeat with the remaining batter.

5. When all the fritters are cooked, serve piping hot.

SERVES 6

NUTRITIONAL ANALYSIS PER SERVING
Calories 229 (Kilojoules 962); Protein 6 g; Carbohydrates 30 g; Total Fat 10 g; Saturated Fat 2 g; Cholesterol 75 mg; Sodium 182 mg; Dietary Fiber 1 g

Caramel Apples with Hazelnuts

1 cup (5 oz/155 g) hazelnuts (filberts)

½ teaspoon salt, plus pinch of salt

6 small green or red apples

½ cup (4 oz/125 g) granulated sugar

½ cup (3½ oz/105 g) firmly packed
light brown sugar

½ cup (5 oz/155 g) light corn syrup

2 cups (16 fl oz/500 ml) heavy
(double) cream

Caramel apples are standard fare at Northwest festivals in the fall. Here's an upscale version made with hazelnuts that's guaranteed to delight both children and adults. If you have any caramel left over after you've coated all the apples, pour it onto a greased baking sheet, let cool, and then cut into squares to make caramel candies.

1. Preheat the oven to 350°F (180°C). Spread the hazelnuts on a baking sheet and toast until the skins are blackened and the nuts are lightly browned, about 15 minutes. Transfer the still-warm nuts to a kitchen towel and rub briskly to remove the skins (don't worry if some flecks remain). Chop coarsely and pour into a small bowl. Mix in the ½ teaspoon salt.

2. Push a popsicle stick into the stem end of each apple, burying it about 1½ inches (4 cm) deep, and set aside. Have ready 6 paper muffin-cup liners.

3. In a deep, narrow, heavy saucepan, combine the granulated and brown sugars, corn syrup, pinch of salt, and cream. Bring to a boil over medium-high heat and cook, stirring constantly, until the mixture registers 250°F (120°C) on a candy thermometer. Working quickly, dip each apple into the caramel, coating evenly and letting the excess drip off. Then dip the end of each apple into the nuts. Place the apples, stick side up, in the muffin-cup liners. Let cool completely before serving.

SERVES 6

NUTRITIONAL ANALYSIS PER SERVING
Calories 695 (Kilojoules 2,919); Protein 5 g; Carbohydrates 77 g; Total Fat 45 g; Saturated Fat 19 g; Cholesterol 109 mg; Sodium 283 mg; Dietary Fiber 4 g

Blackberry Gratin

3 pt (1½ lb/750 g) blackberries, marionberries, boysenberries, or loganberries

½ cup (4 oz/125 g) firmly packed light brown sugar

⅓ cup (3 fl oz/80 ml) heavy (double) cream

1 cup (8 fl oz/250 ml) sour cream

Blackberries seem to grow everywhere in the Pacific Northwest. Unfortunately, the bushes are exceedingly prickly. Before you set out to go picking, protect yourself with long sleeves and heavy trousers, even on the hottest summer days. Pick just enough for this gratin and you'll quickly forget any scratches.

1. Preheat the broiler (griller).

2. In a large bowl, mix together the berries and ¼ cup (2 oz/60 g) of the brown sugar. Pour into a flameproof shallow baking dish or 9-inch (23-cm) pie dish.

3. In a medium bowl, whisk the cream with 1 tablespoon of the brown sugar until soft peaks form. Whisk in the sour cream. Place dollops of the cream mixture on top of the berries, in mounds. Sprinkle evenly with the remaining 3 tablespoons brown sugar.

4. Slip under the broiler about 2 inches (5 cm) from the heat source and broil (grill) until the sugar melts, about 2 minutes. Remove from the broiler and serve immediately.

SERVES 6

NUTRITIONAL ANALYSIS PER SERVING
Calories 257 (Kilojoules 1,079); Protein 2 g; Carbohydrates 35 g; Total Fat 13 g; Saturated Fat 8 g; Cholesterol 35 mg; Sodium 33 mg; Dietary Fiber 5 g

Rice Pudding with Rhubarb-Raspberry Sauce

Jasmine rice, an aromatic long-grain rice, will perfume your entire house as it cooks. Once available only imported from Thailand, it is now grown domestically, too. It pairs well with Asian stir-fries, and makes a lovely rice pudding. You'll need about ½ cup (3½ oz/110 g) uncooked rice to yield 1½ cups (7½ oz/235 g) cooked.

1. To make the pudding, in a large saucepan over medium heat, combine the milk, rice, and sugar. Bring to a boil, stirring frequently, then reduce the heat to a simmer and cook uncovered, stirring occasionally, until thickened, about 45 minutes. Stir in the vanilla, pour into a serving bowl, and let cool.

2. Meanwhile, make the sauce: In a nonaluminum saucepan over high heat, combine the rhubarb, sugar, orange juice, and orange zest. Bring to a boil, reduce the heat to medium, and simmer, stirring occasionally, just until the rhubarb is tender, 10–12 minutes. If using fresh raspberries, stir them into the rhubarb mixture, immediately remove from the heat, and let cool. If using frozen raspberries, stir them into the rhubarb mixture, continuing to stir for 1–2 minutes, or just until thawed, then remove them from the heat and let cool.

3. Serve the pudding and the sauce at room temperature or chilled. To serve, spoon the pudding into individual bowls and pour the sauce over the top.

SERVES 6

NUTRITIONAL ANALYSIS PER SERVING
Calories 298 (Kilojoules 1,252); Protein 7 g; Carbohydrates 56 g; Total Fat 6 g;
Saturated Fat 3 g; Cholesterol 21 mg; Sodium 77 mg; Dietary Fiber 2 g

PUDDING

3¾ cups (30 fl oz/940 ml) milk

1½ cups (7½ oz/235 g) cooked jasmine or other long-grain white rice

½ cup (4 oz/125 g) sugar

1 teaspoon vanilla extract (essence)

RHUBARB-RASPBERRY SAUCE

½ lb (250 g) rhubarb, trimmed and cut into ½-inch (12-mm) chunks

¼ cup (2 oz/60 g) sugar

2 tablespoons fresh orange juice

1 teaspoon grated orange zest

2 cups (8 oz/250 g) fresh or frozen raspberries

Pear Gingerbread

1 tablespoon plus ½ cup (4 oz/
   125 g) unsalted butter, at room
   temperature

1 large, firm but ripe pear *(see note),*
   peeled, cored, and cut into ½-inch
   (12-mm) dice

1½ cups (7½ oz/235 g) all-purpose
   (plain) flour

¾ cup (4 oz/125 g) whole-wheat
   (wholemeal) flour

1½ teaspoons baking soda (bicarbon-
   ate of soda)

1 teaspoon ground ginger

1 teaspoon ground cinnamon

½ teaspoon salt

¼ teaspoon ground nutmeg

1¼ cups (9 oz/280 g) firmly packed
   brown sugar

¾ cup (9 oz/280 g) unsulfured
   molasses

2 eggs

2 teaspoons peeled and grated fresh
   ginger

1 cup (8 fl oz/250 ml) buttermilk

2 cups (16 oz/500 g) plain yogurt

Pears are an important crop in the Rogue and Hood River Valleys of Oregon, and because many of the varieties store well, the fruits are available throughout the year. Anjou or Bosc, both of which have slightly less moisture than many other varieties, will work well in this spicy gingerbread.

1. Preheat the oven to 350°F (180°C). Grease a 7-by-11-inch (18-by-28-cm) baking pan with butter. Dust the pan with flour, tapping out the excess.

2. In a large frying pan over medium-high heat, melt the 1 tablespoon butter. Add the pear and cook, stirring often, until softened, 3–4 minutes. Transfer to a small bowl and let cool.

3. In another bowl, sift together the all-purpose and whole-wheat flours, baking soda, ground ginger, cinnamon, salt, and nutmeg. Set aside.

4. In a separate bowl, using an electric mixer set on medium speed, beat together the ½ cup (4 oz/125 g) butter and ¾ cup (6 oz/180 g) of the brown sugar, until light and fluffy, 2–3 minutes. Gradually beat in the molasses. Add the eggs one at a time, beating well after each addition. Beat in the fresh ginger.

5. With the mixer on low speed, beat the flour mixture into the egg mixture in three batches alternately with the buttermilk, beginning and ending with the flour. Beat just until mixed. Stir in the pear. Pour into the prepared pan.

6. Bake until a cake tester inserted into the center comes out clean, 45–50 minutes. Transfer the pan to a rack and let cool for 15 minutes.

7. While the cake is cooling, in a small bowl, stir together the yogurt and the remaining ½ cup (3 oz/100 g) brown sugar. Cut the cake into squares and serve warm with dollops of the yogurt.

SERVES 8

NUTRITIONAL ANALYSIS PER SERVING
Calories 555 (Kilojoules 2,331); Protein 10 g; Carbohydrates 93 g; Total Fat 17 g;
Saturated Fat 10 g; Cholesterol 98 mg; Sodium 482 mg; Dietary Fiber 3 g

Double Cherry Clafouti

¼ cup (2 oz/60 g) unsalted butter

3 cups (12 oz/375 g) stemmed and pitted ripe sweet cherries (about 1 lb/500 g unpitted)

⅓ cup (1½ oz/45 g) pitted dried sour cherries

8 tablespoons (4 oz/125 g) sugar

¼ cup (2 fl oz/60 ml) kirsch or framboise

3 eggs

⅓ cup (2 oz/60 g) all-purpose (plain) flour

½ cup (4 fl oz/125 ml) milk

1 teaspoon vanilla extract (essence)

⅛ teaspoon salt

1 tablespoon confectioners' (icing) sugar

Clafouti comes from the Limousin region of France, which, like the Pacific Northwest, is an area famous for its sweet cherries. It's a delicious dessert, a combination custard and pancake that traditionally includes whole unpitted cherries. I prefer to omit the pits, using a cherry pitter to speed the task.

1. Preheat the oven to 350°F (180°C). Butter a 9-inch (23-cm) baking dish or pie dish.

2. In a large frying pan over medium-high heat, melt the butter. Add the fresh and dried cherries and 2 tablespoons of the sugar. Cook until bubbling, stirring occasionally, about 2 minutes. Pour in the liqueur and remove from the heat. Cover and set aside for 10 minutes.

3. In a bowl, whisk together the eggs and flour until smooth. Whisk in the remaining 6 tablespoons (3 oz/90 g) sugar, the milk, vanilla, and salt until smooth.

4. Using a slotted spoon, transfer the cherries to the prepared baking dish, reserving the liquid in the pan. Pour the liquid from the frying pan into the batter. Mix well and pour over the cherries.

5. Bake the clafouti until puffed and browned, about 45 minutes. Remove the dish from the oven and let cool on a rack for 10 minutes. Dust the top of the hot clafouti with the confectioners' sugar and serve.

SERVES 6

NUTRITIONAL ANALYSIS PER SERVING
Calories 305 (Kilojoules 1,281); Protein 5 g; Carbohydrates 45 g; Total Fat 12 g; Saturated Fat 6 g; Cholesterol 132 mg; Sodium 92 mg; Dietary Fiber 1 g

In 1847, an oxcart loaded with seven-hundred cherry-tree seedlings traveled the Oregon Trail, carrying the beginnings of the Pacific Northwest cherry industry along with it. Henderson Luelling, a pioneer from Iowa, planted the seedlings in Milwaukie, now a suburb of Portland, and although he later abandoned the state, he left his infant orchard in capable hands. His brother, Seth, cared for the trees and developed two of our most popular sweet cherries, the Bing and the Black Republican.

Today, the Pacific Northwest is renowned for its production of sweet cherries, providing 70 percent of the nation's domestic crop. Thriving on the Northwest mix of warm, sunny days, cool nights, and rich soil, orchards now blanket the Willamette and Hood River Valleys of Oregon and the Okanogan, Yakima, and Wenatchee Valleys of Washington.

Cherries begin ripening in June and continue through mid-August. The leading commercial variety is the Bing, although Van, Lambert, Sweetheart, Rainier, and Royal Ann are also popular.

My own personal favorites come from a truck. Several times a week,

Sweet Cherries

beginning in June, I gather up my family and head for a particular Seattle street corner in search of a pickup marked Ahlberg Orchards Organic Cherries. I buy several pounds, hoping to freeze some for the winter. Unfortunately, most are eaten by the time we enter the house, leaving the car interior decorated with pits and stems.

Apple-Ginger Crisp

8 tart apples *(see note),* peeled, halved, cored, and cut lengthwise into slices ¼ inch (6 mm) thick

½ cup (2½ oz/75 g) all-purpose (plain) flour

½ cup (1½ oz/45 g) old-fashioned rolled oats

½ teaspoon ground cinnamon

¼ teaspoon fine salt

¾ cup (6 oz/185 g) firmly packed light brown sugar

¼ cup (1 oz/30 g) sliced (flaked) almonds

2 tablespoons chopped crystallized ginger

½ cup (4 oz/125 g) chilled unsalted butter, cut up

Newtown Pippin, a favorite cooking apple, has beautiful, bright green skin, taut flesh, and a punching-tart flavor—perfect for this crisp. If unavailable, however, Braeburns or Granny Smiths will give equally good results. Serve this old-fashioned dessert with vanilla ice cream.

1. Preheat the oven to 375°F (190°C).

2. Place the apples in a 2-qt (2-l) baking dish with 2-inch (5-cm) sides. In a large bowl, combine the flour, oats, cinnamon, and salt and mix well. Add the brown sugar, almonds, ginger, and butter and, using a pastry blender or 2 knives, work in the butter until the mixture is crumbly and the butter is evenly distributed. Crumble the flour mixture over the apples.

3. Bake the crisp until the topping is golden brown and the apples are tender, about 55 minutes. Remove the dish from the oven and let cool on a rack until warm.

4. Spoon into individual bowls and serve.

SERVES 6

NUTRITIONAL ANALYSIS PER SERVING
Calories 456 (Kilojoules 1,915); Protein 4 g; Carbohydrates 72 g; Total Fat 19 g; Saturated Fat 10 g; Cholesterol 41 mg; Sodium 114 mg; Dietary Fiber 5 g

Espresso–Triple Chocolate Brownies

½ cup (4 oz/125 g) unsalted butter

4 oz (125 g) unsweetened chocolate, coarsely chopped

3 tablespoons instant espresso powder

2 cups (14 oz/440 g) firmly packed light brown sugar

4 eggs

1 cup (5 oz/155 g) all-purpose (plain) flour

¼ teaspoon salt

½ cup (2 oz/60 g) chopped macadamia nuts

3 oz (90 g) bittersweet chocolate, chopped

3 oz (90 g) white chocolate, chopped

The Northwest's love affair with coffee has been well documented. Great with a latte or a tall glass of milk, these fudgy brownies have a pronounced espresso flavor. If you prefer a subtler kick, reduce the espresso powder to 2 tablespoons.

1. Preheat the oven to 375°F (190°C). Line an 8-inch (20-cm) square baking pan with 2-inch (5-cm) sides with aluminum foil, letting the foil overhang the sides. Butter the foil.

2. In a large, heavy saucepan, combine the butter, unsweetened chocolate, and espresso powder. Place over low heat and stir frequently until smooth. Remove from the heat and stir in the brown sugar until smooth. Then, using a wooden spoon, beat in the eggs one at a time, beating well after each addition. Beat in the flour and salt until combined. Finally, fold in the nuts and the bittersweet and white chocolates just until evenly distributed. Pour into the prepared pan, using a rubber spatula to scrape any batter clinging to the pan.

3. Bake the brownies until they pull away from the sides of the pan, about 40 minutes. Remove from the oven and let cool completely in the pan on a rack.

4. To serve, remove from the pan, using the foil to lift the brownies out, and cut into 16 bars.

SERVES 8

NUTRITIONAL ANALYSIS PER SERVING
Calories 629 (Kilojoules 2,642); Protein 9 g; Carbohydrates 80 g; Total Fat 35 g; Saturated Fat 17 g; Cholesterol 139 mg; Sodium 136 mg; Dietary Fiber 3 g

W herever you are in the Pacific Northwest, whether in a major city or a mountain glen, you're never far from good coffee.

The Northwest's espresso addiction began in 1971, with the opening of the first Starbucks in Seattle's Pike Place Market. Founded by two coffee aficionados, this inaugural spot, modeled after Peet's coffeehouse in Berkeley, California, sold only whole beans until 1984, when espresso drinks were introduced.

Other coffee roasters were quick to follow. Today, large chains such as Seattle's Best Coffee and Tully's Coffee compete with Starbucks, while smaller artisanal roasters such as Oregon's Caravan and Bridgetown Coffee, and Washington's Café D'Arte and Batdorf and Bronson roast the highest-quality beans.

Today, when you step up to the espresso counter, you can order:

Espresso Macchiato An espresso topped with a streak of foamed milk.

Espresso con Panna An espresso topped with a dollop of whipped cream.

Cappuccino An espresso mixed with steamed milk halfway to the rim of the cup, topped with foamed milk.

Espresso

Caffè Latte An espresso mixed with steamed milk almost to the rim of the cup, topped with foamed milk.

Caffè Mocha An espresso mixed with steamed milk, chocolate syrup, and sometimes topped with whipped cream and dusted with cocoa powder.

Caffè Americano An espresso thinned with hot water.

Chocolate-Hazelnut Spread on Toast

½ cup (2½ oz/75 g) hazelnuts (filberts)

½ cup (4 fl oz/125 ml) heavy (double) cream

¼ cup (2 oz/60 g) firmly packed dark brown sugar

½ vanilla bean, split lengthwise

3 oz (90 g) semisweet (plain) chocolate

4 slices artisan bread

2 ripe nectarines or peaches, pitted and sliced

Homemade chocolate-hazelnut spread puts Oregon hazelnuts to excellent use. It is irresistible on toast for a snack or dessert, as it melts and oozes into all the cracks and crevices. Store any leftover spread in the refrigerator for several weeks.

1. Preheat the oven to 350°F (180°C). Spread the hazelnuts on a baking sheet and toast until the skins have blackened and the nuts are lightly browned, about 15 minutes. Transfer the still-warm nuts to a kitchen towel and rub briskly to remove the skins (don't worry if some flecks remain). Place the hazelnuts in a food processor and process, stopping to scrape down the sides several times, until the nuts turn into a paste, 2–3 minutes. Leave the hazelnuts in the processor bowl.

2. In a small saucepan, combine the cream and brown sugar. Using the tip of a knife, scrape the seeds from the vanilla bean halves into the cream. Bring to a boil over high heat, stirring to dissolve the sugar. Remove from the heat, stir in the chocolate, and continue to stir until melted and smooth, about 3 minutes.

3. With the motor running, pour the chocolate mixture into the food processor. Process, stopping to scrape down the sides several times, until the mixture is smooth, about 5 minutes. Transfer to a bowl.

4. To serve, toast the bread slices in a toaster or under a preheated broiler (griller) until golden on both sides and place on individual plates. Pass the chocolate-hazelnut spread and the nectarine or peach slices at the table.

SERVES 4

NUTRITIONAL ANALYSIS PER SERVING
Calories 482 (Kilojoules 2,024); Protein 7 g; Carbohydrates 54 g; Total Fat 29 g; Saturated Fat 11 g; Cholesterol 41 mg; Sodium 193 mg; Dietary Fiber 3 g

Glossary

Barley, Pearl
A favorite ingredient of northern European immigrants to the Pacific Northwest, this mild grain has a tough hull and is polished several times during processing, producing a smooth, pearlescent gray appearance. Good in soups, stews, casseroles, and side dishes.

Beans
Many different beans, both fresh and dried, find favor with Pacific Northwest cooks. Mottled red **cranberry beans,** available dried in well-stocked food stores or fresh in their pods from farmers' markets, are popular in soups and stews or as a side dish. **Fava (broad) beans,** enjoyed for their pale green color and mildly bitter flavor when fresh, may be shelled and then cooked and eaten without peeling when very young and small; shelled and then peeled of their thick outer skins when more mature; or dried and cooked. **Lima (butter) beans,** smaller but similar in color and shape to favas, are found fresh on rare occasions but are most often cooked in their dried form.

Cabbages
In addition to common spherical green and red cabbages, markets throughout the Pacific Northwest and elsewhere now offer two milder types of cabbage that can be enjoyed raw in salads and cooked in stir-fries, soups, and stews. **Napa cabbage,** also known as Chinese or celery cabbage, is distinguished by an elongated shape similar to romaine (cos) lettuce, with thick, crisp white ribs supporting crinkly leaves. **Savoy cabbage,** a mild-tasting European variety, resembles conventional cabbages in its ball-like shape but has wrinkled leaves patterned with lacy veins.

Chile Garlic Sauce, Vietnamese
A dynamite-hot sauce with a pastelike consistency made from chiles and garlic and sometimes labeled Vietnam-style hot garlic sauce or *tuong oi toi Vietnam.*

Chile Paste, Thai Roasted
A richly flavored bottled seasoning paste known in Thai as *nam prik pao.* Do not confuse it with Chinese chile pastes.

Chiles
Popular in Hispanic and Asian kitchens alike, chiles also appear frequently in other interpretations of contemporary cooking in the Pacific Northwest. Three of the most commonly available types used in this book are the **jalapeño,** a plump green or ripened red chile with a fiery flavor; the equally spicy but somewhat sharper-tasting **serrano,** which is small, slender, and also available in green or ripened red forms; and **Thai chiles,** which resemble serranos in size and heat but are slightly more elongated, with pointed tips.

Clams
The cold waters of the Pacific Northwest host a wealth of clams, among which the best known are **Manila clams,** also known as Japanese littlenecks, recognizable by their black-striped shells and enjoyed for their sweet, tender flesh. The **local littleneck,** also known as the butter clam, is a sweet, tender variety with a shell barely more than 2 inches (5 cm) across at its widest point. When cleaning clams, discard any that do not close when tapped.

Coconut Milk, Unsweetened
Sold canned or frozen in Asian markets and used as an enrichment in many Southeast Asian recipes, this rich-tasting liquid is made by grating fresh coconut

meat and combining it with hot water, then straining out the particles from which all the milky essence has been extracted. If left undisturbed, a thick layer of **coconut cream** will have risen to the surface of the milk. Shake well before opening to blend the cream into the milk, or lift off the cream for a lower-fat milk. Avoid sweetened "coconut cream," commonly used as an ingredient in tropical cocktails.

Daikon

This long, white Japanese radish has a refreshingly hot-sweet flavor and crisp texture. It is grated or thinly sliced raw for use in salads, tempura dipping broths, or noodle dishes; cut into slices or chunks and cooked in stews and broths; or sliced and pickled.

Dungeness Crab

Taking its name from a town on Washington's Olympic Peninsula but harvested the entire length of North America's Pacific Coast, this crustacean is prized for its sweet flavor and firm texture and is generally acknowledged to yield some of the continent's best crabmeat. Distinguished by the red-and-cream color of their shells, the crabs have bodies that average 9 inches (23 cm) across. Washington law permits the harvesting of specimens as small as 6¼ inches (15.5 cm), while some Dungeness crabs are as large as almost a foot (30 cm) across. For the best flavor, purchase live crabs and cook them the same day.

Fennel

Enjoyed for its sweet, mild anise flavor, this plant comes in two forms used in distinct ways in the kitchen. **Florence fennel**, also known as Florentine or bulb fennel, is a bulb vegetable, and its crisp

greenish white flesh is eaten raw or cooked. **Common fennel** is a variety grown specifically for its frilly, dark green fronds, which are a seasoning primarily for seafood. Fronds trimmed from Florence fennel may be used in the same way.

Fish Cheeks

These small pockets of flesh from the head of a fish—most commonly salmon or halibut—are considered by some to be the tastiest part of the fish—a special treat. Today, salmon cheeks are less readily available in markets than

Cheeses

BLUE, OREGON

In the southwestern Oregon town of Central Point in the 1950s, cheese maker Tom Vella began making Roquefort-style blue cheeses with a culture he carried back from a trip to the famed French region. Today, Oregon blues are prized for their savory but not overly salty character and their smooth, soft texture. Substitute other mild to moderately flavored blue cheeses.

CHEDDAR, SHARP

Because of its pastureland, the Northwest produces excellent cheddar-style cheeses, of which the most renowned are two made in Oregon coastal towns: the hand-turned, hand-pressed cheddars of Bandon, in the south, and the better-known yellow cheddars produced from raw milk by the Tillamook County Creamery Association in the north.

GOAT, FRESH

Often referred to by the French term *chèvre* and enjoying a steady growth in demand, this creamy, tangy cheese is being made by a number of producers in the region, among which is Mt. Capra in Chehalis, Washington, which uses raw goat's milk.

PARMESAN

The best of this type of firm, nutlike, salty-tasting Italian grating cheese is generally acknowledged to be Parmigiano-Reggiano, produced from cow's milk mid-April to mid-November in a region that embraces Parma, Modena, Mantua, and Bologna, and aged for at least 14 months. For the best quality, buy Parmesan in block form, selecting pieces with a good, deep yellow color and even, grainy texture; grate it fresh, just before use.

PECORINO ROMANO

Typically used in its aged form for grating, this popular Italian cheese resembles Parmesan but has a sharper, tangier flavor, a result of the sheep's milk from which it is made.

Greens

Greens from around the world find their way into the produce departments, farmers' markets, and home gardens of the Pacific Northwest.

ARUGULA
Also known as rocket, these small, notch-edged leaves have a mildly bitter taste and tender texture that can be appreciated raw in salads or briefly cooked.

BOK CHOY, BABY
Juicy and crisp, this variety of Chinese cabbage is also known as Shanghai bok choy. The small heads can be separated into individual leaves and stir-fried, sautéed, braised, or simmered in soups.

BROCCOLI RABE
Distinguished by deep green leaves on slender, sturdy stalks crowned by small florets, this popular Italian green is also commonly referred to as broccoli raab, rape, or *rapini*. It has a crisp texture and a refreshing edge of bitter flavor.

GAI LAN
A Chinese relative of broccoli, these long, leafy stalks, with their small clusters of white blossoms, have a refreshing crunch and slightly bitter taste. Serve them sautéed or stir-fried as a side dish.

MIZUNA
Also known as Japanese mustard, this sweet-sharp, fernlike, spiky little leaf adds spicy flavor and crunchy texture to salads and may also be quickly stir-fried or steamed. It is often included in prepackaged salad-green mixes.

PEA SHOOTS
The sweet, tender baby leaves and tendrils of the snow pea, these are enjoyed raw, steamed, stir-fried, or simmered in soups.

SORREL
A sharp, lemony flavor distinguishes these elongated green leaves. When very young and mild in taste, they may be included in salads. Otherwise, sorrel leaves are best cooked in soups, sauces, or stuffings, during which they break down into a puréelike consistency.

WATERCRESS
Part of the mustard family, this wild or commercially cultivated green has a refreshing crispness and a peppery bite that is welcome raw in salads or as a garnish or cooked in soups.

halibut cheeks, which can be purchased fresh or frozen throughout the Pacific Northwest. Approximately the size of sea scallops, halibut cheeks are excellent roasted or sautéed.

Fish Sauce
Made from salted and fermented fish, this thin, amber liquid plays a role in Southeast Asian kitchens similar to that played by soy sauce in China and Japan. Depending upon their country of origin or manufacturer, fish sauces vary in taste and intensity but are generally interchangeable. Thai fish sauce is known as *nam pla,* Vietnamese fish sauce as *nuoc mam.*

Five-Spice Powder
A popular Chinese commercial spice blend commonly composed of star anise, Sichuan peppercorns, cloves, cinnamon, and fennel seeds.

Hoisin Sauce
Chinese bottled seasoning based on fermented soybeans and seasoned with vinegar, garlic, chile, sesame oil, and other ingredients. Prized for its thick consistency and savory-sweet flavor.

Lingcod
Although its name may suggest otherwise, this northern Pacific fish is not a member of the cod family but is a variety of greenling. An unattractive creature that nonetheless has outstandingly sweet, mild-tasting, firm, lean flesh, lingcod can be cooked by virtually any method.

Mussels
Sweet-tasting native blue mussels thrive in the rocks and pilings along the Pacific Northwest shore. These wild mussels are available in food stores; however, most

mussels in the marketplace today are farmed. Cultivated mussels tend to have a more delicate flavor, thinner, shinier black shells, and less sand or grit to deal with than their wild counterparts. Before cooking, mussels must be debearded, that is, the tough filament by which they cling to surfaces must be pulled off. On cultivated mussels, the beards tend to be very small and easy to remove. When cleaning mussels, discard any that do not close when tapped.

Port, Northwest
Several wine makers in the region are now producing domestic versions of this classic Portuguese fortified red wine, savored for its sweet flavor and full body.

Potatoes
The cool climate of the Pacific Northwest is ideal for growing potatoes. Among the most popular varieties is the **russet,** also known as the Idaho or baking potato, a large, brown-skinned type with a dry, mealy texture ideal for roasting, deep-frying, or mashing. Several varieties of thin-skinned, yellow-fleshed, waxy-textured potatoes have won a following for their rich flavor and their versatility in the kitchen. Among them are **Yellow Finn** and **Yukon gold,** which can be steamed, boiled, mashed, roasted, or sautéed. In farmers' markets, keep an eye out for so-called **heirloom potatoes.** These distinctive varieties, with intriguing shapes, sizes, and colors, disappeared from widespread distribution decades ago because they did not lend themselves to commercial cultivation, but enterprising small-scale growers have been reintroducing them to the marketplace.

Rice Vinegar, Unseasoned
Clear, clean-tasting vinegar made from rice wine, used to add bright flavor to sauces, salad dressings, and pickles. Unseasoned varieties allow home cooks more latitude in seasoning dishes to taste, while seasoned versions contain salt and sugar. Japanese rice vinegars tend to be milder in flavor than those from China.

Scallops
The sweet, succulent, disk-shaped muscles of these bivalves make a popular appetizer or main course when quickly cooked by sautéing, stir-frying, deep-frying, or poaching. Large Pacific **sea scallops** are harvested in tidal ponds and coves along the continent's northwest coast from Oregon to Alaska. The **singing scallop,** also known as the pink scallop for its lovely pink-and-white shell, thrives in the waters of Puget Sound. Also popular with local cooks are tiny **bay scallops,** which are harvested in Atlantic waters.

Sesame Oil, Asian
Oil pressed from toasted sesame seeds, producing a dark amber color and a rich, nutlike flavor and aroma that make it a prized seasoning. It is added to sauces or drizzled over dishes toward the end of cooking. Do not use it alone for frying. Buy the oil in small quantities and store covered at cool room temperature, as it tends to go rancid quickly.

Shallots
Relatives of the onion, these small brown-skinned bulbs with purple-white flesh are popular as a seasoning. Some people describe their flavor as a combination of onion and garlic.

Smelts
Slender, glimmering silver-skinned fish about the size of large anchovies, smelts are usually panfried or deep-fried and eaten whole, or gutted and smoked. Two types, **eulachon** (Columbia River smelt) and **whitebait,** are caught in the Pacific Northwest and are at their best from winter to midspring, when they head upriver from the ocean to spawn. The Chinook used to dry eulachons, thread wicks through them, and burn them like candles, the source of their nickname, candlefish.

Tamari
A type of Japanese soy sauce made without the wheat that traditionally accompanies soybeans in the fermentation process. It has a thicker consistency and stronger flavor than ordinary soy sauces. Look for it in health-food stores.

Umeboshi Plum Vinegar
Commercial seasoning derived from the brine left behind in the manufacture of Japanese *umeboshi,* or pickled plums. The fruits are picked while still green and are pickled in a brine seasoned with shiso, an herb that gives them an astringent flavor and pale pink color. Used in dressings and sauces, the vinegar is nonacidic, mild, and fragrant.

Walnuts and Walnut Oil
Native to the Middle East, **walnuts** were brought to the Pacific Coast by Spanish friars in the late-18th century. The nuts lend themselves to many robust dishes of the Pacific Northwest. Walnuts in their shell will stay fresh for 3 months or longer; shelled, they should be stored in an airtight container, where they will keep for up to 12 months in the freezer. To enhance the taste of dishes containing walnuts, or to add a touch of walnut flavor without the crunch, use a little **walnut oil,** pressed from lightly toasted nuts. Buy it in small quantities and store airtight in a cool, dark place, as the oil can go rancid quickly.

Index

Acknowledgments

Jean Galton wishes to thank Val Cipollone and Sarah Lemas of Weldon Owen for their vision and plain old hard work. She also wishes to thank her wonderful husband, Ron Pellegrino, for contributing healthy amounts of research and editing and for introducing her to the Pacific Northwest.

Leigh Beisch wishes to thank Chehalem Vineyard and Schand Knox Filbert Farm, Newberg, OR; Hurst's Berry Farm, Sheridan, OR; Pike Place Market, Seattle, WA; and the Walla Walla Onion Commission. She also wishes to thank The New Lab and Pro Camera, San Francisco, CA, and FUJI Film for their generous support of this project.

Weldon Owen wishes to thank the following people and associations for their generous assistance and support in producing this book: Desne Border, Ken DellaPenta, Dana Goldberg, Chris Hemesath, Annette Sandoval, Kate Sullivan, and Hill Nutrition Associates.

Photo Credits

Weldon Owen wishes to thank the following photographers and organizations for permission to reproduce their copyrighted photographs:
(Clockwise from top left) Pages 14–15 : Jeffrey Braverman; Dave Perry/Ecostock;
Terry Wallace/Ecostock; John Kernick; Leigh Beisch; Bruce Forster/Viewfinders; Brooke Slezak
Page 16: Robin Cushman; Michael Melford; Steve Bly; Dave Curran
Page 42: Lisa Romerein; Beth Beljon; Beth Beljon; Jeffrey Braverman; Robin Cushman
Page 82: Josh Paul; Dave Perry/Ecostock; George White; Ron Cronin/Ecostock
Page 114: Dennis Frates; Leigh Beisch; Dave Perry/Ecostock; Brooke Slezak; Leigh Beisch

Time-Life Books is a division of Time Life Inc.

Time-Life is a trademark of Time Warner Inc.,
and affiliated companies.

TIME LIFE INC.

President and CEO: **Jim Nelson**

TIME-LIFE TRADE PUBLISHING

Vice President and Publisher: **Neil Levin**

Senior Director of Acquisitions
and Editorial Resources: **Jennifer L. Pearce**

WILLIAMS-SONOMA

Founder and Vice-Chairman: **Chuck Williams**

Book Buyer: **Cecilia Michaelis**

WELDON OWEN INC.

Chief Executive Officer: **John Owen**

President: **Terry Newell**

Chief Operating Officer: **Larry Partington**

Vice President International Sales: **Stuart Laurence**

Associate Publisher: **Val Cipollone**

Editor: **Sarah Lemas**

Copy Editor: **Sharon Silva**

Consulting Editor: **Norman Kolpas**

Design: **Jane Palecek**

Production Director: **Stephanie Sherman**

Food Stylist: **Dan Becker**

Prop Stylist: **Sara Slavin**

Studio Assistant: **Sheri Giblin**

Food Styling Assistant: **Michael Procopio**

Scenic Photo Research: **Caren Alpert**

The Williams-Sonoma New American Cooking Series
conceived and produced by Weldon Owen Inc.
814 Montgomery Street, San Francisco, CA 94133

In collaboration with Williams-Sonoma
3250 Van Ness Avenue, San Francisco, CA 94109

Separations by Bright Arts Graphics (S) Pte. Ltd.
Printed in Singapore by Tien Wah Press (Pte.) Ltd.

A WELDON OWEN PRODUCTION

Copyright © 2000 Weldon Owen Inc. and
Williams-Sonoma Inc.
All rights reserved, including the right of
reproduction in whole or in part in any form.

Map copyright © Ann Field

First printed in 2000
10 9 8 7 6 5 4 3 2 1

Library of Congress
Cataloging-in-Publication Data

Galton, Jean.
The Pacific Northwest / general editor, Chuck Williams;
recipes and text, Jean Galton; photography, Leigh Beisch.
p. cm. — (Williams-Sonoma New American Cooking)
ISBN 0-7370-2045-8
1. Cookery, American--Pacific Northwest style.
I. Williams, Chuck. II. Title. III. Series.
TX715.2.P32 G35 2000
641.59795— dc21   00-024944
CIP

A NOTE ON NUTRITIONAL ANALYSIS
Each recipe is analyzed for significant nutrients per
serving. Not included in the analysis are ingredients
that are optional or added to taste, or are suggested
as an alternative or substitution either in the recipe
or in the recipe introduction. In recipes that yield
a range of servings, the analysis is for the middle
of that range.

A NOTE ON WEIGHTS AND MEASURES
All recipes include customary U.S. and metric
measurements. Metric conversions are based on
a standard developed for these books and have
been rounded off. Actual weights may vary.